Why the
Gospel of Thomas
Matters

The Spirituality of Incertainties

Why the *Gospel of Thomas* Matters

The Spirituality of Incertainties

Gethin Abraham-Williams

Includes the *Good as New* Translation
of the *Gospel of Thomas*

CHRISTIAN
ALTERNATIVE

Winchester, UK
Washington, USA

First published by Christian Alternative Books, 2015
Christian Alternative Books is an imprint of John Hunt Publishing Ltd.,
Laurel House, Station Approach,
Alresford, Hants, SO24 9JH, UK
office1@jhpbooks.net
www.johnhuntpublishing.com
www.christian-alternative.com

For distributor details and how to order please visit the 'Ordering' section on our website.

Text copyright: Gethin Abraham-Williams 2015

ISBN: 978 1 78279 929 0
Library of Congress Control Number: 2015932895

A CIP catalogue record for this book is available from the British Library.

Design: Stuart Davies

Printed in the USA by Edwards Brothers Malloy

We operate a distinctive and ethical publishing philosophy in all areas of our business, from our global network of authors to production and worldwide distribution.

CONTENTS

For our granddaughter
Isabelle Anne

who is discovering the importance of incertainties

Why the *Gospel of Thomas* Matters

Gethin Abraham-Williams, an Oxford University graduate in Theology, is a Baptist minister, and a Cardiff University tutor in Christian Beliefs. In 2006 he was awarded the Cross of St Augustine by the Archbishop of Canterbury for 'making an enormous contribution to ecumenical relations through broadcasting, publications and active participation.'

In this artfully written and engaging book, Gethin Abraham-Williams brings a wealth of experience and research to the task of weaving a contemporary spirituality marked by incertainty from the rich and paradoxical strands of the Gospel of Thomas. In doing so he takes us on a highly rewarding reflective journey through the world of the (five) Gospels, via Nag Hammadi, to contemporary South Wales and war-torn Syria with numerous other stops in between. The interplay of theology, history and contemporary experience generates much food for thought and spiritual life, with particularly rich insights for inter-faith dialogue and inter-spirituality. This is a truly ecumenical book that is as happy gleaning insight from other faith traditions as from different traditions of Christianity, including those long buried; a deeply pastoral book full of spiritual wisdom.
Revd Dr Stephen Roberts, *Senior Lecturer in Modern Theology, University of Chichester.*

Passionate, poetic and political, Gethin Abraham-Williams' reflection on the Johannine Thomas, the Gospel attributed to him and the challenges we face to live faithfully within a changing world affirms the apostle's 'incertainties', confronted by something as transformative, crazy even, as resurrection. Rightly rejecting the 'doubting' label, it models for us beautifully the importance for spiritual maturity of an enquiring mind.

Revd Dr Anne Phillips, *Spiritual accompanist and former Co-Principal, Northern Baptist Learning Community.*

In this book Gethin Abraham-Williams provides a fresh look at an old Gospel which still has something to say to a postmodern world. While he treats the extra canonical Gospel of Thomas with both respect and academic discipline, comparing and contrasting its claims with those of the canonical Gospels, his primary interest is in gleaning key insights that have relevance for our time. Central among these insights is Thomas' 'incertainty', his unwillingness to accept secondhand faith claims or to profess any belief he does not genuinely hold. Abraham-Williams *demonstrates in practical* ways how 'incertainty' (a term borrowed from a Shakespeare sonnet) is neither an obstacle to faith nor even a prelude to faith but rather an essential companion of any genuine faith.

Revd Dr Christopher Chapman, *First Baptist Church, Raleigh, North Carolina.*

I really enjoyed this book. I loved the mix of personal stories and the arts (literature, poetry etc.) to illustrate some deep theology, which is itself expressed in a lucid manner. Gethin Abraham-Williams has written a book that is interesting, challenging, and insightful. He uses a fascinating text (the Gospel of Thomas) that most of us have heard about, but many of us know little about, to shed light on how our faith relates to today's global, multicultural world.

Revd Dr Trystan Owain Hughes, *Christian theologian, historian and author.*

Gethin Abraham-Williams breathes life into the Gospel of Thomas in a way none before him have dared, and where a less masterful guide could only stumble. I can no longer read this mysterious gospel as an obtuse collection of random sayings; I've now been exposed to it as a heart-rending quest for truth and purpose. He quotes various sayings in the Gospel of Thomas (it is not a narrative gospel like the others, but a collection of Jesus' sayings), as translated by John Henson in his *Good as New* publication. Henson's translation makes for fun reading, and matches Gethin's captivating writing style. The two of them form a partnership that brings this oft-maligned 'doubting apostle' alive before our eyes. Thomas, insists Gethin, "may be the least understood but arguably the most original of all the disciples. [...] He can no longer be written off as little more than a foil to the Apostle Peter's certainties. Now he exists in his own right as a key witness to the teaching of Jesus and as the apostolic spokesperson for a much more radical stream among the disciples."
Lee Harmon, *'John's Gospel: The Way it Happened'*.

I cannot remember precisely, what led me to include 'Thomas' in *Good as New*, but whatever it was I came to the decision to 'fly a kite'. I am, therefore, exceedingly grateful to Gethin Abraham-Williams for revealing why the inclusion of Thomas among the Christian scriptures is a 'must'.
John Henson, *New Testament translator.*

By setting selected sayings from the Gospel of Thomas alongside the disciple's own words from the Fourth Gospel, this book challenges the myth of 'doubting Thomas', arguing that 'incertainty' is an essential element of any authentic faith experience.

In an age of increasing anti-Semitism and religious intolerance, it also affirms the importance of the Gospel of Thomas in recovering the essential Jewishness of Jesus.

Far from undermining the Christian tradition of the Church and its canonical scriptures, this book shows how the Gospel of Thomas complements both, inviting the reader to reconsider the healthy significance of the Apostle of the Enquiring Mind.

The last in the author's *Spirituality Trilogy*, after:

Spirituality or Religion? Do we have to choose?
&
Seeing the Good in Unfamiliar Spiritualities

Incertainties now crowne them-felves affur'ed
Shakespeare, Sonnet 107, 1609 Quarto version

Preface

WHEN THE GOSPEL of Thomas was discovered at Nag Hammadi in Upper Egypt in the middle of the last century, it led to a flurry of academic interest and Biblical research.

Since then, the Gospel of Thomas has been quietly gaining an appreciable degree of scholastic acceptance as a Fifth Gospel, worthy of being received and studied alongside the other four gospels as part of the on-going life, witness and devotion of the Christian church.

The Gospel that Thomas is credited with writing, reveals a much more Jewish Jesus than is obvious from the four canonical versions. It is full of sayings to startle us into a fresh awareness of how controversial Jesus was and of what was required of those who would follow him.

I am aware of only one version of the New Testament currently available that includes a translation of the Gospel of Thomas alongside that of Matthew, Mark, Luke and John, and that is: *Good as New: A Radical Retelling of the Scriptures* by John Henson, published in hard and paperback by O-books (2004), which is the text I have used throughout. There are other versions of the Gospel of Thomas on the market, but as free-standing translations, some of which I have cross-referenced.[1]

In the canonical Gospels of Matthew, Mark and Luke, Thomas is no more than a name. It's the Fourth Gospel that gives him any kind of a voice, and then only towards the end and in a handful of tantalisingly unamplified interventions. Even so those interruptions are consistent with and substantiated by the approach taken by the Gospel of Thomas which increases the probability of the Gospel of Thomas being the genuine article.

My contention is that for too long Thomas has been thoughtlessly regarded as no more than a byword for doubt in a wholly negative aspect, whereas as I read him, and as I detect from the

'Sayings' of Jesus he recorded, doubt for him was a much more positive attribute. I have tried to capture this ambivalence by using the old English word '<u>incertainty</u>', rather than the more usual 'uncertainty'. Shakespeare uses it in one of his sonnets, and it seems to me to be a much more positive word than the 'uncertainty' into which it evolved in later usage. It's also much better fitted for describing the kind of concerns and issues which occupied the faithful disciple Thomas, and which I believe resonate more closely with current attitudes towards religion in general and Christianity in particular.

Far from undermining the Christian tradition of the Church and its canonical scriptures, the Gospel of Thomas complements both, and invites us to reconsider the healthy significance of the Apostle of the Enquiring Mind!

1 Who was Thomas?

He appointed twelve to be his companions and to be sent out to proclaim the gospel, with authority to drive out demons.[2]

'WHO ON EARTH was Thomas?' seems to be a wholly unnecessary question. Thomas was Thomas, one of the Twelve: an astute northern lad, from a northern town; his northern accent belying an acute intelligence.

The southern sophisticates in and around Jerusalem, couldn't entertain the notion of anything worthwhile coming from a region that felt more Roman than Jewish. Along the elegant colonnades of Galilee's provincial capital, Sepphoris, barely four miles from Nazareth, the philosophy of the Cynics now challenged the certainties of the Torah.

Even the surrounding landscape, rocky and rugged, where Barak had overcome Sisera in the days before they had kings, tended to breed a type inured by climate and continuous conditioning from taking anything at face value. This was an ambiguous borderland between the deeply entrenched Judaism of the south and a necessary and longstanding accommodation with generations of Phoenician and other settlers: a Galilee of the nations.[3] The region had spawned too many mystical philosophers and miracle workers for most of its inhabitants to be anything other than sceptical in the face of facile solutions and unsubstantiated panaceas.

'Who was Thomas?' only becomes an intriguing question, because we have this so called Fifth Gospel: the Gospel of Thomas (GofTh). The question would never arise otherwise. In the Fourth Gospel (the Gospel of 'John'), the few times Thomas is listed as contributing to the story, he's always referred to as Thomas, and nothing but Thomas. And in the list of disciples in the other three Gospels, he's just Thomas. But in the very first

'Saying' in his own Gospel he is at pains to tell us that Thomas is not his name, Thomas is his nickname, and his real name is Jude or Judas!

> *Here is a collection of some of (Jesus') most intriguing and challenging sayings, passed on by one of his closest friends, whose real name was Jude, but better known by his nickname, Twin.* (GofTh 1)

The nickname is all the more puzzling because he not only affirms it but underlines it, stresses it, by saying it twice: once in Greek, once in his native tongue. '*I, Didymus – Judas – Thomas*' have collected and arranged these Sayings and am passing them on: 'I'm Thomas, the Double, the Twin'. Even that might not matter so much if it weren't that the meaning of the nickname is in itself ambiguous! There are, of course, other examples in the Gospels of prominent figures being re-named by Jesus when they became his followers. The fisherman Simon is re-named Peter, the rock; the prosecuting Pharisee, Saul is re-named Paul after his Damascus Road conversion. Thomas though is different.

Thomas in one form, Didymus in the other: the one Greek, the other Aramaic, both meaning 'twin', each a direct translation of the other. In any language 'Twin' is an odd nickname to give anyone, because the implication is always that to refer to anyone as a twin is to do so in relation to the other similar or identical twin. And if so, who?

Some have cast Thomas in the role of twin to Jesus. A Jude (or its variant, Judas), to whom the New Testament letter of Jude is attributed, is certainly named among the brothers of Jesus listed in the Gospels.[4]

Or is the nickname just the recognition of a longstanding friendship? Of Thomas and Jesus as inseparable boyhood mates, whose relationship had kept pace with the passing of the years? Was that what lay behind his claim to be one of Jesus' 'closest friends'? – because they'd gone to the same synagogue, become 'sons of the Commandment', been bar-mitzvahed, on the same day? Or – if the legend of Thomas in later life working as an architect in the Indus valley[5] is to be believed – because he'd served his apprenticeship, side by side with Jesus in Joseph bar-Jacob's carpentry shop in Nazareth; a rough, tough craft where physical strength and endurance mattered, and the tang of sawdust anointed the plane and the lathe.

If that is the case, what could be more natural than that Thomas had learned the rudiments of architecture, and which timber was best for a beam and which for a frame – the oak or the cypress, the cedar or the ash; or sandalwood and teak from the far east – in the shop at Nazareth? Running his coarsening fingers along the smooth surface of the planed planks, had Thomas, perhaps, also traced in the pattern of the grain, in the knots and the seams, the lineage of a tribe, the span of a life, and the cost of cutting against the grain? In the shop at Nazareth, had Thomas learnt the art of dissembling when soldiers came calling with orders for crosses, in return for a fistful of denarii?

Or might there be another explanation? According to one scholar[6], the laboured repetition of the name, first in Aramaic and then in Greek, is nothing less than a device for drawing attention to the fact that Jesus was a teacher in the Wisdom tradition of Proverbs and of the book of Ecclesiasticus, where the meaning of a saying is found with reference to its double.

In that case, if for no other, the Gospel of Thomas is a useful addition to the narrative versions of the four evangelists, in that it captures, in both content and form, the way Jesus probably spoke and taught, making 'Thomas' less of a name and more of 'a kind of code word expressing a truth in the wisdom tradition'.

The teaching of Jesus, as recorded in the Gospel of Thomas, certainly gives us an insight into a style that is startlingly different when compared with similar sayings in the other four gospels. For that alone the Gospel of Thomas matters, because it introduces us to a Jesus we thought we'd understood, but might not have.

> Jesus said, 'You've enjoyed listening to the many things I've had to say to you. I've told you what no one else can tell you. Make the most of the opportunities you have to get my advice. There will be times when you won't be able to get hold of me.' (GofTh 38)

The Jesus we encounter in these Sayings is, undoubtedly, the product of a uniquely Jewish world which became submerged quite early on as the good news of Jesus was re-interpreted for a Hellenistic culture and a Latin empire. Was it to stem that tide that Thomas recalled a particular Saying of Jesus that emphasised the importance of Jesus' brother James as the keeper of the tradition when he was no longer with them? This was James the Just, who became a leader in the Jerusalem church and was respected as the custodian of an authentically Hebraic interpretation of his brother's teaching.

> The friends of Jesus said to him, "We know you're going to leave us. What shall we do for a leader?" Jesus said, "If you have any problems, you can always go to my brother James for advice. He's honest and fair. I think the world of him!" (GofTh 12)

So the nickname 'Thomas' may be any of a number of things, including a reference to a boyhood friendship, or a literary device for flagging up the need to recognise the distinctive Jewish style of the teaching of Jesus.

It might, however, be a hint of something else, of a shared secret, between him and Jesus; something it would be too risky, too controversial to divulge too soon; an intimation that Thomas might have discerned something that went beyond messianic expectations and had ventured onto dangerous theological territory. That Jesus might not just have been a teacher 'in the wisdom tradition', but somehow have also been its personification. That his humanity needed interpreting in the light of divinity, and that in Jesus divinity had been encountered in flesh and blood.

> *Then Jesus took Twin to one side and had a serious chat with him. When they joined the other friends again they said, 'What did he say to you?' Twin said, 'If I tried to tell you, you'd kill me ...!' (GofTh 13b)*

In the Biblical book, the Wisdom of Solomon, wisdom is described in terms which implies a pre-existent 'spirit' that comes from God, who is also one with God, and through whom all things came to be: 'the flawless mirror of the active power of God, the image of his goodness.'[7]

The very name 'Thomas', may, therefore, be intended as a clue, not only how to read the Sayings of Jesus, but more important, how to read Jesus himself, with apparently contradictory Sayings 'twinned' to bring out a deeper, a more profound theological meaning. If that is the case, Thomas may be the least understood, but arguably the most original, of all the disciples.

To immerse oneself in the Gospel of Thomas, therefore, is a little like attending a modern Passion Play. It requires a suspension of existing assumptions in order to allow a different reality to take centre stage in one's spiritual exploration. It's a delving into a sequence of apparent contradictions in order to discover if and how they can be complementary. It's about the incertainties of faith as a necessary process towards authentic discipleship. Might a Passion Play I witnessed one Easter weekend, provide a key to unlock the complexity of this intriguing Gospel and the disciple who assembled it?

'Who are you exactly?'

It was as close to the familiar narrative as you'd expect, with all the usual characters, but with a clever, dramatic twist. It was a study in ambiguity that challenged conventional interpretations. Like the Gospel of Thomas, by stripping away the narrative, it confronted us with a Jesus who is both challengingly direct but also infuriatingly oblique!

> Jesus said, ... 'It's true that in the past I sometimes dodged your questions. Now that I'm offering you the answers, you've lost your curiosity.' (GofTh 92b)

The Christ in the play I saw was a teacher, not a rabbi, and a teacher who didn't teach or preach. He listened. He listened to everyone. All the time. Especially to those whom no one had been listening to for too long to remember.

At the moment of the dying of this Christ on the cross, his last words were not: 'It is finished', or any of the other six recorded sayings, but: 'I remember'. Just that. 'I remember,' remembering for all the people who'd forgotten, forgotten their past; whose stories had been lost and with it their own identities. And in resurrecting their stories, the teacher's own lost story of who he was and where he'd come from had come flooding back. A collective redemption triggered by his own surrender to the brutal noise that had crowded out the healing memories. It perplexed me at the time, because it was – it seemed – uncannily close to the original, and yet it wasn't. Or was it?

When the scholars began deciphering the codex that we know as the Gospel of Thomas they were equally puzzled. Was the figure that emerged from this one hundred and fourteen apparently haphazard collections of Sayings, the same as the teacher, preacher, miracle-worker familiar from the four gospel accounts in the New Testament collection?

Does the Gospel of Thomas matter, not because of its similarities to sayings in the familiar gospels, but because of its differences? Because it startles us into awareness that we might not, after all, have got Jesus taped: doctrinally signed, sealed and delivered.

The people listening said, 'Who are you exactly? How can we trust you when we don't know anything about you?' (GofTh 91a)

Is not the danger with all religious systems that they want to systematise spirituality too neatly, to do it so successfully that it loses its freshness, its capacity to disturb and surprise, to release the spirit?

Though there is no narrative of the Passion as such in the Gospel of Thomas, it is there in the Sayings, and because of that it comes upon you almost unawares. It's there in Sayings like the following:

Jesus drew the attention of his friends to someone from another country who was on the road to Jerusalem and carrying a lamb. Jesus asked them, "Why has he got the lamb tied up?" They said, "Probably because he means to kill it and have it to eat." Jesus said "He won't get any food from the lamb until he's killed it." (GofTh 60a)

The Gospel of Thomas is Christianity's Second Opinion. It confirms the original by restating the original, only differently. And that's what the Passion Play I saw had aimed to do.

The play, in being different, in updating the story to give it, as it were, a local make-over, a contemporary relevance – was it, though, still the same story? Perhaps that's the wrong question. That's the question that springs from the need for reassurance, for corroboration of one's certainties, for release from further engagement. The better question is the one Thomas never asks directly in his Gospel, but whose answers he gathers up in his verbal baskets, one hundred and fourteen of them, like grains of wheat.

Was it still the same story – of heaven brought down to earth, of a death that liberated, of a tapping into a contemporary spirituality that cannot grasp the concept of salvation, of being saved from, only of being saved for; not of being found, but of being able to find for oneself, where even the original Girl Guide pledge to God and the Queen is now deemed passé, and substitutes a promise to 'be true to myself and develop my beliefs'.

Jesus said, "If anyone asks you, 'Where do you come from? Where do you get your ideas? You should reply, 'We come from the light which appeared at the beginning of all things. That same light made us what we are.' If they ask you, 'Are you the light itself?' you must say, 'No, we're only children of the light, people who know the living God as our parent.' And if they ask you, 'What evidence can you give us of your family likeness to God?' say, Like God we're always on the move and always at rest.'" (GofTh 50)

The first-century Passion is imprinted on our imaginations. Its horror both attracts and repels us. Even the most irreligious will stand in silent awe at a re-enactment of the crucifixion. The Christian claim that in this one victim God was somehow victimised, baffles, but also intrigues us.

The Passion Play I witnessed wasn't Oberammergau. It was in an industrial town on the South Wales coast. It took place in the open air over three days between one Good Friday and an Easter Sunday. At its peak the audience topped twelve thousand, who watching, became incorporated willingly or otherwise into the story. We were all collaborators in the end. Mute witnesses to injustice, to a lost present.

The London critics watched it too and wrote it up. They came because the lead was being played by Hollywood actor, Michael Sheen. They came because of him, but they stayed on because of the story.

What had brought Sheen to this town in industrial decline?

The steel industry that had once transformed this sleepy, beautiful sandy bay into a 'treasure island' of prosperity, of re-housing and re-settlement, of new clubs and pubs, of new schools and a big hospital, was now in recession. The steel giant, Corus (since acquired by the Indian conglomerate, Tata), was pulling back. Its stubby towers were still belching out their thick promising smoke, but less iron was being smelted to be poured, and cooled, mangled and rolled, to satisfy the world's demands for steel. Other places could make it cheaper. And the coal to fuel the furnaces was no longer coming from the rich seams of the South Wales valleys – it was being shipped in ignominiously from outside in an act of industrial effrontery, because the valley mines had been run down in a fight to the death between Westminster and the Unions. And the Unions had lost.

The Hollywood star came to this place because this was the place that had named and nurtured him. And because he'd remembered, as a boy, watching the town perform an annual open air Passion Play. Sheen had been shaped by the place. 'I grew up on the hillside overlooking the town proper,' he remembers. 'On a good day you could look out across the sea and glimpse the English coast, on a better one you only saw Port Talbot. The chemical plant cooling towers stood imperiously before me, turning the sky orange and spitting acid at the washing and the cars. The steelworks on fire and smoking "Woodbines". And always the sea, washing up its whales and submarines, failed kites and once reaching out with its roiling hand across the beach road and stealing away a child, never to be seen again in spite of all the car headlights.'[8]

The town had changed in the meantime. So the story had to change. Not in its outline, not in its cast of disciples and high priests, of Roman soldiers and palm-waving cheerleaders, but in its relevance.

As a boy of 12 Sheen had been introduced to the idea of a Passion Play as a local institution performed annually in the grounds of a wooded park on the southern slopes of Mynydd Margam, a mile or two to the east. 'I saw it a few times over the years until it stopped being done,' he remembered. 'It was a story I knew come to life in front of me. A ritual taking place before me. I saw the people of my town walking out of the forest and out of another time, children dancing and the old walking with their lost [sic], following the man who had come back. The man who had been on a strange journey, who had suffered, had visions, and who returned.'

Sheen wanted to recapture the impact of that memory for a new generation, almost to create a secular passion, as if the first passion hadn't been secular, as if the secular now could free itself from resonances of that first passion. 'Something had been called to that place and was still there as we left.'

Jesus said, 'I've set the world on fire. I must keep fuelling it until there's a good blaze!' (GofTh 10)

This, therefore, had to be a particular story: a story of this particular town – built like Venice on stilts in the soft sand of the coastal seabed, to carry the heavy machinery, the cooling towers, the transport infrastructure and the housing to re-settle the established inhabitants, whose intimate homes had once leaned into their dependable terraces of mutual support and irresistible gossip. Most of the terraces were long gone, razed to their forgotten foundations to make room for the factories and the concrete pylons supporting the noisy new motorway, overshadowing them, like another, later 'Passover'.

This would have to be a story of a lost way of life, of a lost sense of community from earlier times when an expectation of generational continuity was not unreasonable. This would have to be a Passion that would restore a surrendered respect, the rediscovery of individual and communal worth.

So the Hollywood star and a young Welsh poet, Owen Sheers,

were brought together under the auspices of the innovative National Theatre Wales to recreate a Passion with all the power of the original, but anchored in a present reality: 'The Gospel of Us'[9], it was called, with a message that salvation is in the remembering here and now, not in some imagined heaven, but on the tarmacadamed highways of the world, from South Wales to South America, from the post-industrial West to the newly industrialised cities of the burgeoning East.

It was an attractive scenario. It was a clever take on the old, old story that seemed to rescue the story, whose metaphysics a post-religious age is unable to buy into, whilst relating its plot lines and its pathos to its inherent promise of some sort of resurrection. It was not quite the 'Jesus is alive!' of the Gospel of Thomas' confident new morning, less of life beyond death, rather of a life snatched back from a numbing, soulless present, to be a life with some degree of quality restored, to be lived through and lived out now. 'Something about a town telling a story to itself,' Sheen explained. 'A town remembering itself through a story. Sacrifice. Betrayal. Denial, Love. Passion.'

'Too bright for our eyes'

Thomas might have felt at home with much of this, but how far might he have identified with what was going on here, between a Friday yet to be and an Easter beyond his present grasp? Would the disciple who represents the incertainties of faith, who reserved judgement on the Jesus who'd called his friend Lazarus back from the deadness of his cavernous tomb, have entered into the idea of 'a town telling a story to itself'? Would the Thomas, who at the last supper, had wanted to know that there was some substance behind the soaring words, that it was all leading somewhere, for them, for his occupied nation, have seen the value of 'a town remembering itself through a story. Sacrifice. Betrayal. Denial. Love. Passion'? And after it was all over to have sorted through all the sayings and collected the ones that illustrated the story best and arranged them in sets, brick upon brick, layer upon layer in a way that described his own painful pilgrimage towards accepting the incertainties of faith as the secret to revive desiccated disciples thirsting after illusory certainties?

> *Jesus said, 'It's impossible to know what God looks like. The sight is too bright for our eyes. But God's character can shine through human beings.'* (GofTh 83)

Perhaps God's character does shine 'through human beings', and more than we realised as we watched this latter day Passion. The 'Do this in remembrance of me' that Thomas heard at the last supper was never meant to be a lover's fond farewell, the hope of a condemned man that he'd not be forgotten. It was to be a folding-in of time. A Dr Who moment. A catapulting of a life of eternal significance into everyone's present. A 'proleptic' experience, something existing before its proper time that we were nevertheless already allowed to see in representational anticipation.

For Wolfhart Pannenberg, the prominent German Protestant theologian, writing in the second half of the 20th century, that was the only way a post-Christian, post-Modern generation could grasp the significance of the Jesus event.[10] The last chapter in the evolution of humankind has already been written, the last reel filmed, he argued, and we've been given an advanced copy as it were, a preview, in the story of Jesus.

Was this what the Port Talbot Passion portrayed? Because there was certainly a resurrection moment. The story was not over with the dying on the cross, which, even in re-enactment, was profoundly disturbing. I hid from the worst of it in a nearby café. I needed the anaesthetising of coffee to cope. I took myself out of the next to last scene. I fled from the garden. I made myself inconspicuous in the wings of this thunderously soul-churning drama. I opted for out.

The crowd on the seafront that balmy Easter Sunday evening was made of sterner stuff. They stuck it out. Families, dads holding the hands of children, little ones 'cwtched' in the folds of their mothers' arms, grandparents in sober stillness, gauche teenagers caught in uncomfortable seriousness.

'If you don't make the Rest Day a day free from life's stress, you won't be in the right frame of mind to meet with the Loving God.' (GofTh 27b)

The history teacher was crucified on a seafront roundabout by night, his brother singing him to death in a forgotten language, itself little more than a memory to many of the current Anglicised generation, an affirmation in itself of a twinned people with a dual identity in an increasingly monoglot world, singing of Dafydd (David of the White Rock), asking for his harp so that he might play one last tune on it: '"Cariwch", medd Dafydd, "fy nhelyn i mi,/Ceisiaf cyn marw roi tôn arni hi./Codwch fy nwylo i gyrraedd y tant."'

And if this was God? Surely the ultimate incertainty of spirituality? And if this was man? It echoed the secret Thomas struggled over, as he too once stood at the foot of a cross, one in which real nails were hammered through sentient flesh.

But there is a resurrection scene. 'It has begun', says the figure in the afterglow of the setting sun beside the empty cross. It has begun.

To what extent are we justified in using this modern Passion to interpret the ancient, Fifth Gospel, and equally, to use the Gospel of Thomas to test the interpretive achievements of this clever, unique Passion, so beautifully staged and sensitively acted over three days on a multitude of different platforms in familiar locations? Gospel scenes re-created in normal settings from a popular beach to a bustling shopping mall, from a parish church graveyard to a seaside Labour Club, throbbing with the music of the cult status, alternative rock band, the Manic Street Preachers – famous for songs of alienation, boredom and despair.

The play certainly gets close, so very close, to a contemporary take to what the original story was about; and which, in being so close, might somehow have been too close to capture the reality of a spirituality that transcends the story while being unashamedly earthed in it. Incertainties sometimes elude representation. Addressing Salome, who's been a close follower throughout his ministry, and who's listed in Mark's Gospel as one of the women disciples 'who had followed him and looked after him when he was in Galilee'[11] and was there at the last, at the foot of the cross:

> *Jesus said, 'To understand the things I say, you need to use your imagination.' (GofTh 62a)*

The central figure in the Port Talbot Passion was a teacher who'd gone missing from home, who unexpectedly turned up one day on a crowded beach, where the locals had been corralled for a civic event. Had he come from the sea, or from beyond the sea? From Galilee or from beyond the Gower? Whatever past the teacher had, he had forgotten it – a kind of kenosis, a self-emptying – and was now forever listening to other people's stories of their forgotten past.

And we the watchers, what had we forgotten of our past? Stories of faith that provided a framework for believing, that stretched the imagination because they touched on real experience. That helped us earth our separate identities. That we passed down from one generation to another in wall paintings and hymns, in scripture lessons and pointed homilies, in private devotion and homely studies, in lived lives, lived differently, because the stories had enlarged the internal canvas of our lives, giving it shape, providing models that matched what we felt to be true and honest, just and pure, lovely and of good report.[12]

'You just can't see it'

So the plot moved on to its appointed climax. And the corrupt authorities in this imagined totalitarian utopia that was the context for this modern Passion, moved in for the kill. It was expedient that one man should die for the people rather than for a whole town to be wiped out. So the teacher who listens is silenced, and in the very act of dying, he remembers who he is, who he was, and it all comes tumbling out in the names and the places that had softened their lives and reminded them of the pleasure they'd once had in and with each other. And the teacher's remembering is a trigger for the people's remembering what they once had, before they'd become a treasure island, before the steel plant was built and the ugly, overbearing overpass.

Under a now darkened sky on a seaside promenade one Easter Sunday evening, they lowered the teacher's body from the cross, 'lowered him like a flag, his body loose and heavy into the lap of his mother', while one of the women, who stood vigil, sang a lullaby: 'So sleep on now, come take your rest/The hour is soon to come/Behold us now, for it is night/We'll rise again at dawn.' – as they covered and wrapped him up.

But they wanted to take one last look: his mam to stroke his hair. So they loosened his shroud, only to find he'd gone! 'And in his place were flowers'. It was as if 'someone had planted a spring meadow inside him,' was how Owen Sheers described it in his script, 'and now, with his death, it had taken bloom.'

And when his followers looked up at the empty cross, suddenly 'there he was ... Bold as brass. He looked over us all staring up at him, and then he spoke to us. "It has begun!" he said. And then he was gone.'

It's an attractive scenario. And it's a lot cleverer than many contemporary re-enactments of the original. It's clever to turn a preacher into a listener, a rabbi into a disciple, because people who are listened to are more likely to recover a sense of their own worth. And as drama it worked, and as a community building project it worked, and in terms of the local boy turned Hollywood star it worked. But in terms of that elusive thing that is spirituality, the Gospel of Thomas captures it better.

Better – because it exposes the incertainties of the Christian 'myth', and thereby its persistent appeal as a faith that stretches credulity to its limits and somehow thereby becomes believable.

> *The friends of Jesus asked him, 'When will those who have died be at peace, and when will God's New World come?' Jesus said, 'It's all happened already; you just can't see it!'* (GofTh 51)

This idea of being at peace, at rest, resonates with the preceding Saying of Jesus where he talks of God, like himself, 'always on the move and always at rest'. And it occurs again a little later where the idea is of a 'secure hide-out', and the context is clearly the Passover, and of events in the Garden of Gethsemane:

> *Jesus said, 'If you have no wish to give yourselves for the life of others, like a lamb, you'd better find yourselves a secure hide-out. There's no security in making yourself comfortable with a friend on a sofa. At any moment one of you may be taken out for execution and the other spared.'* (GofTh 60b)

Was this what Thomas was doing in this Gospel? Stripping away the narrative till all we are left with is nothing but raw dialogue, or more often monologue? No storyline, just spoken words remembered – like a script from the theatre of the absurd: 'Krapp's Last Tape'; 'The Chairs'; 'Waiting for Godot', 'The Homecoming': Ionesco, Beckett, Pinter.

'Christ is contingency,' says the poet, Christian Wiman. 'Contingency. Meaning subject to chance, not absolute. Meaning uncertain, as reality, right down to the molecular level, is uncertain. As all of human life is uncertain. I suppose that to think of God in these terms might seem for some people deeply troubling (not to mention heretical), but I find it a comfort. It is akin to the notion of God entering and understanding – or understanding that there could be no understanding (*My God, my God, why has thou forsaken me?*) – human suffering. If Christianity is going to mean anything at all for us now, then the humanity of God cannot be a half measure.'[13]

The tantalising question, 'Who was Thomas?' is, therefore, bound up with the larger, more intriguing question of 'Who was Jesus?' And the answer to both is neither as simple nor as transparent as Christians and others have sometimes maintained – nor as Thomas has often been misrepresented as implying.

2 What did Thomas doubt?

Unless I see the mark of the nails ...[14]

THOMAS DIDN'T DOUBT, he questioned, and that's a very different matter. Nowhere in the New Testament is Thomas described as doubting. Rather he's described as questioning, and in particular questioning the claim of the other disciples that Jesus, whom he'd seen crucified, dead and buried, was somehow alive. 'Unless I see the mark of the nails on his hands, unless I put my finger into the place where the nails were, and my hand into his side, I will never believe it.'[15]

We underestimate the sense of failure and desolation the disciples must have felt following the crucifixion. Before they knew otherwise, the depth of their despair must have been terrible. Endlessly going over what had gone wrong, why it had happened, and what was to become of them now. 'On the day after his death Jesus was no hero, saviour, or redeemer,' the late Alan E Lewis reminds us in his remarkable study: *Between Cross & Resurrection*.[16] 'He is dead and gone, convicted as a sinner, a rebel and blasphemer, who has paid the price of tragic failure. He simply died, and his cause died with him, quite falsified and finished.'

On the evening of the Sabbath following the Thursday-Friday executions one can imagine the little, dejected band of faithful followers cowering from the authorities in the upper room of a safe house somewhere in Jerusalem. Thomas wasn't there. He'd gone off on his own to try to work out in his own mind why it had all gone so horribly wrong. Maybe he was skulking along the slippery streets of Zion in some kind of shattered torpor, stunned by the inconclusiveness of the whole preposterous escapade. Whatever the reason he wasn't there with the rest when it happened.

Jesus said, 'Make your life a quest and don't give up till you find what you're looking for.' (GofTh 2a)

And that's what Thomas had done, or at least tried to do – to make his life a quest. Trying to remember now if he'd missed something:

– like the time they'd been at a wedding with Jesus, where the wine had run out. A happy affair: the streets and alleyways round the synagogue in the little town of Cana in Galilee alive with laughter and singing and dancing; and the elders remembering their own weddings, and telling stories, and the young couple under the 'chuppah' sharing the one cup before the groom smashed it to bits under his foot, and family and friends had all cheered. There'd been other weddings they'd gone to, but he remembered that one because the wine and the water jars had got mixed up. Not enough wine. Looking back it was as if wine and water was a theme running through their time with the dead rabbi. And numbers too. Six water jars, twelve disciples. Why six? It had all seemed so natural at the time. No call to try to find a meaning in it. Not then. But now it was different.[17]

– or when they'd gone back to Cana weeks later. Called on the couple, saw how happy they were. Teased the embarrassed chap whether a baby was on the way! Then this Roman had turned up and everybody had gone tense. An officer in a cohort stationed in nearby Nahum. A garrison town. A reminder of occupation, of loss of sovereignty. And every Shabbat they'd pray for Messiah to come to restore what was lost. The soldier said he had a lad he was fond of who was ill: his boyfriend, by all accounts. Unnatural practices. Needed condemning. Immoral lot the Romans. The superstitious soldier had heard our Galilean rabbi had the healing touch.

Could he do something, perhaps? Jesus shouldn't have had anything to do with him. They all agreed on that, disciples and villagers. Whatever the rabbi did, the story spread that the boy had recovered. Thomas couldn't understand why there'd been no condemnation! He tried to understand now, but maybe it was too late with Jesus dead and buried.[18] Were these events at Cana clues? And if so, what did they mean?

When Thomas caught up with the rest of the friends later, they told him all about what he'd missed – the ultimately incredible event of a three-year-long roller coaster of mind bending instances, ideas, insights and improbabilities; of confrontations, conversations, confusions and catastrophes – and he'd missed it! The climax, the divine intervention to beat all interventions. The ultimate showdown. What he'd been looking for all the time. The denouement. And he, Thomas Didymus, had chosen that very moment to be absent, to be out of the room, to be gone on a walkabout to clear his head, to nurse his disappointed hopes.

They'd come to Jerusalem from time to time. Jesus seemed drawn to the place – more's the pity. Told them his parents had taken him there for his bar mitzvah. This time they were there for Shavout, or was it for Yom Kippur? Anyway, the blind, the lame, the paralyzed were all sitting round the pool near the temple as usual, waiting for their own individual exodus, waiting to catch the waters when they bubbled with life, rattling their begging bowls for a passing coin or two. Then Jesus cottoned on to one of these old fellows, leaning against one of the five arches. Finds out he's been stuck there 38 years! Numbers again – and water. Another clue? Anyway Jesus hoiked him up on his feet, or I think that's what he did, and wonder of wonder, he didn't fall over! Didn't need to get baptised, Jesus told him! Off home he toddled, apparently none the worse for wear! It was Shabbat, though. Wasn't necessary to do it on Shabbat. Could have waited till later. Thomas wasn't surprised the authorities didn't like it. And now this.[19]

"We've seen the Leader!" the friends told him. For Thomas, though, that wasn't good enough. "I won't believe that until I see the holes made by the nails in his wrists and put my finger into them. And I'll have to examine his side too!"

He'd been part of the rabbi's story for most of that remarkable ministry. Thomas' questions hadn't suddenly come to a head when it all went wrong, they'd been building up gradually over the months and the years. He'd always been one to keep his opinions to himself until he was sure enough to share them, which was rare. Even as a boy in Nazareth, Thomas had been relieved when others had voiced the awkward question, and uncommitted when easy answers were offered. He'd never been one to take things at face value, always turning things over in his mind, listening.

'I won't believe it – until, or unless, or except that I see for myself and touch for myself.' Thomas didn't trust other people's experience, not because he didn't believe them. He was perfectly prepared to acknowledge that what they were telling him was what they genuinely felt they'd experienced. He wasn't questioning their integrity. But he wasn't the sort of person either who's prepared to take secondhand experiences on board. He needed his own authentic encounter, or nothing at all.

Popular usage has saddled Thomas with the word 'doubt' – 'Doubting Thomas': that he 'doubted' what other people told him – even his most trusted friends, the group he'd been with through hell and high water. But that's not fair on Thomas. The word 'doubt' is not there in the Fourth Gospel account anyway. For Thomas, 'faith' was too important a concept to say he had it, when he knew that 'having faith' was not some hand-me-down item of clothing you put on if you'd nothing better to wear. It was something you really wanted, and knew, beyond a shadow of doubt, when you'd found it. It was the culmination of a process, a succession of insights, ideas and life experiences, coming together, early or later, to re-arrange the pattern of one's perceptions ever after. The when and the wherefores might fade beyond recall, and the battling with its implications prove never-ending, but the memory would persist, that once, in the deepest recesses of one's emotional intelligence, a change had come about.

Thomas questioned that anything he hadn't experienced could be relevant to him. Thomas, we are told, was eventually allowed to see. What to make of that, how to interpret it will have to await a later chapter. Inevitably, our modern interest is in that 'resurrection appearance', and how to understand it.

'Blessed are those who have not seen and yet believe.' The rebuke, attributed to the resurrected Jesus is specifically addressed to Thomas in the Fourth Gospel. As such it has been taken as implying a particular shortcoming in Thomas, rather than as an encouragement to future generations to understand and interpret resurrection as a matter of insight rather than physical sight. Similar expressions are found in the other gospels, some far more forceful and addressed to all of the disciples. In one particularly memorable instance, Jesus is remembered expressing his frustration with all his disciples. 'What an unbelieving generation!' he says, on hearing that none of them had had enough faith to heal an epileptic boy. 'How long shall I be with you? How long must I endure you?'[20]

It is because the Fourth Gospel specifically casts Thomas as the lone carrier of this important message that the myth of 'Doubting Thomas' was born, and with it the implication that there's something pathetic if you are always having to question your faith – whereas the theological importance of Thomas is the very opposite. Here was a disciple, one of the original Twelve, at the very heart of the movement, for whom the credibility of faith depends, not on its certainties, but on its 'incertainties' – a far better word than the more usual 'uncertainties'. Without the Gospel of Thomas we might never have realised how integral such an approach was to the teaching of Jesus and to the life of faith. And without its chance discovery in the middle of the last century it might never have come to light.

'May upset your prejudices'

It was towards the end of 1945 CE that several Egyptian peasant farmers were riding their camels near the Jabal al-Tarif, a huge cliff that flanks the Nile River in Upper Egypt not far from the modern city of Nag Hammadi. In Professor Marvin Meyer's description, 'they were looking for sabakh, a natural fertiliser that accumulates in the area ... so they hobbled their camels at the foot of the Jabal al-Tarif' – and began to dig around a large boulder that had fallen on the rocky debris that had accumulated at the foot of the cliff.[21]

It was probably Abu al-Majid, the youngest of the al-Samman clan, who unearthed the jar – a large, reddish, airtight pot. Hesitating to break it open for fear it housed a mischievous jinn, thoughts of hidden treasure eventually overcame their superstitions, and Abu's older brother Muhammad Ali brought down his mattock, smashing the pot to bits. Instead of the treasure haul they'd hoped to find, all it contained was a stack of apparently worthless old books: twelve leather-bound papyrus codices.

An antiquarian would have realised their value immediately, handling them with care, lifting each one out carefully with gloved hands. Not so the weather-beaten fingers of these Arab peasant farmers. As they scrabbled through the contents and divided the brittle leaves among those of their number who felt they might be worth trading for a few oranges in the local market, covers fell off, pages got mixed up, and bits were left behind to wither and decay in the dry dust and the scorching sun.

Muhammad knotted his share of the books in the cloth of his unwound headdress, slung the bundle on his shoulder, untethered his camel, and made for home, where he dropped them down casually beside an open fire, where more pages were damaged and lost. The texts taken by the other farmers fared no better.

Enough of the pot's literary treasures, nevertheless, survived, and were eventually recognised for what they are: a collection of manuscripts dating from the third and fourth centuries and written in the Coptic language, though the works were probably all translations from Greek, the best known of which is the Gospel of Thomas. It was a discovery that 'came as a bombshell to the historical and theological communities' of that post-war world. The codices are now housed in the Coptic Museum in Cairo. Fascinating as is the story of the discovery of these ancient codices, fifty-two of them in all, the story of why they were hidden away in this way is even more intriguing.[22]

They probably belonged to the nearby Pachomian monastery from a time when Christianity was struggling for survival in the face of an extremely popular alternative religious system, which drew on passages from the New Testament selectively and misleadingly. Gnosticism's fundamental weakness was its denial that God, who was good, could have been directly responsible for a creation which it regarded as inherently bad. Redemption of the human spirit thus lay in acquiring the secret knowledge which the Gnostics alone claimed to possess.

The struggle between the two movements continued over numerous decades, and it may have been to avoid the plunder and destruction of their precious library by an increasingly confident church during bishop Athanasius' fourth-century purge, that the monks of St Pachomian decided to hide their literary treasures in the earth nearby.[23] And there they lay forgotten until a chance dig by an Arab lad brought them to light in the middle of the last century.

A church that had endured repeated persecution, and had recently become main-stream following the patronage of the emperor Constantine, was in no mood to tolerate deviants. Incorporation by the state, however, had its down side, and during a period of conflicting and contradicting theological arguments over who Jesus was and what Jesus meant, the result was widespread intolerance.

That the Gospel of Thomas had been found among a set of mostly Gnostic treaties was, however, enough initially for the scholars studying the Hammadi collection to brand Thomas' Gospel as non-orthodox by association. Today, however, it is largely accepted that the Gospel of Thomas is of Christian origin, and of considerable Christian importance, not least for the light it throws on a disciple whose identity seemed for so long to elude us only to fascinate us because it suggests so much more than in the throwaway epithet: Doubting Thomas!

With the discovery of his gospel, Thomas can no longer be written off as little more than a foil to the Apostle Peter's certainties. Now he exists in his own right as a key witness to the teaching of Jesus and as the apostolic spokesperson for a much more radical stream among the disciples. Thomas was probably part of an early tradition of reflective believers, which spawned two very different but lasting gospels: the Fourth Gospel and the recently unearthed Gospel of Thomas. But without the Gospel of Thomas we might never have known the full extent of that meditative tradition, nor of the sheer provocativeness of some of Jesus' less well-known sayings. What the Gospel of Thomas does is to bring out the teaching of Jesus with startling sharpness which it achieves because there is no narrative. We are given the Sayings unadorned, without any gloss or interpretive aside. We are left to react to the Sayings without any commentary.

> *Jesus said ... You're fond of saying, 'You can't preach to a dog or teach a pig a lesson.' Make sure those words don't apply to you!* (GofTh 93)

This Jesus jumps off the page to challenge and disturb our settled spiritualities. This Thomas is the companion of our endless searching for spiritual satisfaction. 'Unless I see ...' It resonates with those genuinely wanting to believe, and it echoes the scepticism of those for whom faith is a vain repetition of unsustainable superstitions.

There's a line in one of the detective novels of Donna Leon that I find I cannot get out of my head, because I think it is profoundly wrong! 'We pass through centuries, and we learn nothing,' her fictional hero, the Commissario Guido Brunetti concludes as he investigates a case of deception and gullibility in modern-day Venice.[24] Brunetti cannot see the difference between what he calls the Catholic mumbling of the priest at a funeral mass, putting evil spirits to flight, and the pagan rituals of ancient Rome. But there is a significant difference, and it is the capacity to discern between what is life-enhancing and life-denying. It is the ability to appreciate the difference between a religion that is self-delusional and a faith that is illuminating, between reading the signs of the times and reading the signs of stars. What we need to be deeply suspicious of is a fundamentalism that brooks no argument or a ritual that becomes the object rather than the means of revelation. What is critical is to tell the difference.

> Jesus said, 'What you find may upset your prejudices, but you'll discover much to wonder at and get to grips with what the world is all about.' (GofTh 2b)

In the current religious trough that we seem to be in, in the west at least, insufficient weight has been given, certainly within the Christian tradition, to the fact that among the inner circle of the disciples of Jesus, later to be ennobled as 'apostles' – those specifically sent out to announce the New Age, there was at least one disciple whose instinct it was to hesitate in the face of anything that seemed not to make sense, or to fly in the face of reason, or was downright unbelievable!

The story of doubting Thomas has been passed on and passed down the ages without that all important caveat, that belief is a critical process, and that far from questions being tolerated, they're a positive attribute – for why else would Thomas' interjections into the smooth running of the Gospel narrative from the early ministry of Jesus to his death on a cross have been included in the tradition and not excised from it?

These Thomasine interjections are there at the heart of the narrative for one very important reason, namely that to question is not a failure of moral fibre but the very stuff out of which true religion is fashioned. To question is not an unfortunate trait that afflicts the feeble minded, but a sign of intellectual rigour that gives faith its moral force. The Gospel of Thomas endorses the quest for truth as a vital part of a living spirituality. It is there in some measure in other New Testament writers too. 'Don't pour cold water on the efforts of others or sneer when they're passing on messages from God,' the Thessalonians were warned. Think carefully about everything they say, then hang on to what makes sense.'[25] 'Unless I see, until I feel ...' needs repatriating, not as a term of derision or as a challenge to exercise greater determination in finding the incredible credible, the incertain certain, but as a moral imperative that enriches rather than demolishes faith.

'What you see and can't see'

There was, therefore, certainly an element of resistance in assuming that other people's experiences could ever be enough to satisfy Thomas' quest. Faith by proxy was not an option he could live with, or live by. But there was more to Thomas' objection, 'Unless, until I see ...' than a wariness of a secondhand spirituality.

He was also questioning the very meaning of the life they'd lived as followers of Jesus. What had it all been about? Especially as it had all come to such a shameful end? It hadn't just petered out, it had come to a cataclysmic end. Crucifixion was a pretty terrible fate for even the worst of criminals. But in this context crucifixion was far worse. It felt as if God, the God of Abraham and Sarah, of Isaac and Rebecca, of Jacob and Rachel; the God of Moses, who'd given them the Torah, the God of the Prophets, of Amos and Hosea, of Ezekiel and Isaiah, the God of their wonderful, charismatic, inspiring Jesus, had just withdrawn from the whole amazing, Messianic project. What had it all been about? What had he, Thomas been doing thinking it was ever going to work? What did his life amount to? Where was its meaning?

Questioning the meaning of life is what we all do when life shudders to a standstill, or shows signs of falling apart: when illness intrudes, or redundancy, or war, or natural disaster, or an accident, or loss; that's when we stop and think and ask the big questions. And the time most of us ask the biggest question of all is when death breaks across the smooth running of our lives, the death of a loved one, or an awareness of how finite our own lives are.

There is a particular poem by Dylan Thomas which has embedded itself in popular culture and sometimes surfaces in commemoration services. It is Dylan's elegy to his dying father: 'Do not go gentle into that good night'. What is less known is that he later wrote another version of this poem, after his father's death and when he was himself becoming more aware of his own mortality.

In the first, the tone is defiant, urging his blind, stroke-struck father to 'rage, rage against the dying of the light'. Seven years later, among his unpublished papers, another version was found. Defiance has now given way to a quite different, more speculative, even sombre mood. This time he does not urge his father to 'rage, rage against the dying of the light'. Rather he remembers praying, 'let him find no rest but be fathered and found,/I prayed in the crouching room, by his blind bed ...'[26]

In the hope to be 'fathered and found', were there echoes perhaps of a lost religious culture that had not only shaped Dylan's writing and outlook, but that of a bygone era? Like that of my grandmother Mary Jane's generation. My mother's mother had died long before I was born, but the family remembered that hers had been a 'living faith' and a 'religion of the heart'. In the last stages of cancer, aged 57, with her husband and four children gathered round her bed, she had said with quiet confidence, and they had heard it with similar expectancy, 'I'll be waiting for you all – and Dad will receive the first welcome.'

In more evangelical circles today that kind of certainty will still be common, but I am thinking here of the general Christian culture of the present age, and it is in a different place in matters of faith and religion from where it was, even when I was growing up. I sense an unspoken struggle to find the language that allows us to be positively incertain.

Time has passed for us to conceive of life everlasting as natural. Our culture is in transition, reluctant to completely release its hold on religion however tenuous; hesitant to accept the finality of our mortality, but equally hesitant to deny it. 'Unless I see ...'

Jesus said:

'Everything that now exists will change – what you see and can't see. Being alive or dead has nothing to do with breathing and nothing to do with corpses.' (GofTh 11a)

My friend, David, was someone who was forced to consider the meaning of 'everything that now exists will change', when in early retirement he was diagnosed with an inoperable cancer. David had a logical, practical mind and brought to his thinking a detachment that enabled him to talk about its consequences for him, for his wife, and their grown-up son and daughter, with remarkable candour.

One of the things that struck him, he said, after a lifetime of listening to sermons, was how little preaching he'd heard about death and dying. Persuaded to put his thoughts and feelings in writing, he wrote an amazingly honest article, pointedly entitled, 'Sod's Law, not God's Law'. Eventually published in a church monthly magazine which had softened his title to, 'Parting Thoughts',[27] it was nonetheless challenging in terms of its contents.

In the conversations we had following the announcement of his diagnosis, I was eager to know what, from his unique, if unwelcome vantage point in 'God's Waiting Room', he thought awaited him after he'd shaken off this mortal coil?

Here was a deeply committed Christian, a conviction Baptist, and a lay preacher of many years' standing. His answer broke with convention. 'My problem', he said, 'is that, although I hear in the Christian gospel a clear invitation to believe in a life to come, I do not find it possible in any conventional sense to believe it. In the past I have sometimes tried to persuade myself that I believed it, but deep down I knew I didn't. … if I'm wrong and find myself after death confronted by a chorus of more orthodox friends singing, "I told you so," I will of course be delighted. But I don't expect it.'

David was someone for whom death was not something to be speculated on in a general way as part of our common lot, but of someone of great integrity and honesty facing his own death, believing that 'being alive or dead has nothing to do with breathing and nothing to do with corpses'. For David the concept of a conscious continuity beyond death and outside time was not on, other than as a completed book in God's library, the final cut of the film of one's life for release into God's eternal present. Since God is, by definition, outside time, David argued, his life in its entirety from conception to expiry, and at any and all points in between, would always be 'present' to God, for God to 'access', along with everyone else's life, as God may choose.

For someone with his background to express his 'parting thoughts' so candidly was to my mind brave and probing, and there was no doubt there were many who were helped by it, because his point of view was not a denial of the beliefs that had sustained him personally, as well as in his professional life as a theological educator and in his church commitments, but an update of their meaning. His was an acceptance of the limitations of trying to say anything more about our lives than that we have lived, well or ill, or most often somewhere in between. Less to 'win glory before death,' in the sense of the old Beowulf saga, as to accept that whatever remains of one's life, 'when a warrior is gone/that will be his best and only bulwark.'[28]

For David, the Apostle Paul and the Fourth Gospel in particular have over influenced the development of Christianity when it comes to conceptualising 'the life of the world to come'. So he conceived of God as one for whom our different and diverse existences exist as some kind of living archive, to be reviewed at will but never to be interacted with.

If, however, God's essence, in some imponderable but essential sense, is relational, does that not imply a journey with and in God – and by implication with others – that is more than finite? And if, as the old catechism states, our chief end is 'to enjoy God for ever', might it not hold a kernel of truth that what is begun here and now, does not end here and now?

'What the New Testament writers have in common is not a set of beliefs or doctrines, but a person – Jesus of Nazareth', David amplified in a subsequent comment on his article. 'I want to see today's Christians join that biblical conversation,' he wrote, 'and struggle to work out what they believe, safe in the confidence they, too, have in their Lord.' Thomas couldn't have put it better!

My conversations with David, and with others facing death and prepared to be similarly honest in their incertainties, left me reflecting on how difficult it is for people, good people, caring people, in a culture where 'unless, until I see …' is such a powerful element, to be able to give expression to thoughts and feelings that are not so easily explained. Is it so hard to imagine that we might, just might, be more than the ash that is left when our bodies have been cremated, only to live on in the memory of our loved ones and in whatever opportunities we've had to pass on our genes?

As Paul Fiddes, Professor of Systematic Theology in the University of Oxford, comments in a superb collection of essays in a recent book entitled, Baptists and the Communion of Saints, 'to be remembered by God is a quantum leap forward from being in the memory banks of a computer, or even being remembered by a fellow human being … God is not, after all, a giant monistic mind, but a communion of relationships, and the image of memory only points to being held within the interweaving movement of these relations of self-giving love.'[29]

There is so much more to 'being alive or dead' than breathing or corpses, as that Saying of Jesus affirms. The monotheistic constructs of the Abrahamic faiths, are not temporary scaffolding to be dismantled now that the building blocks of hard facts are in place, but the very walls themselves. They are not chocks placed on a runway until the aircraft of human endeavour is ready for take-off, to be kicked away to let the magnificence of human achievement take to the skies, but the wind that provides the lift.

How long will it be before we reclaim these big faith narratives that have been honed by the great religions through countless generations, not because we cannot face the truth of our own mortality, but because they contain timeless and indispensable insights and revelations that we need if our human achievements and discoveries are not to render us a brilliant but mechanistic species?

'Let them shape your personality'

David's initial reaction to being told he'd only so many months to live had been to question, 'Who we are once all the constructs we create to give ourselves meaning have been stripped away'.

The question could as easily apply to Thomas, unwilling to believe something he himself hadn't experienced, and equally unwilling to believe, because others believed. But beyond either of these legitimate responses, there lay the suspicion that he had yet to face the only question that really matters to any of us: 'Who are we once all the constructs we create to give ourselves meaning have been stripped away'?

Thomas was into authentic experience, and he was also the sort of person who thought deeply about the meaning of life. He questioned everything in his quest to find what he was looking for. Ultimately, though, the 'Unless, until, I see, touch' had more to do with his own inner incertainties. He questioned – himself. Was he Thomas, or was he Didymus? Was he neither, or was he both? It is a question the bereaved most often raise, and Thomas was inconsolably bereaved.

David's diagnosis had made him face the reality, he said, 'of what has our life been about when we are in a position to look back on it with any degree of objectivity.'

Jesus said:

'Ideas come to life when you let them shape your personality.'
(GofTh 11c)

I once posed a similar question to a medical friend, 'Why am I here?' I asked Iain during one of our more meandering conversations, fortified by Bloody Marys and various lethal concoctions! And he, unable to resist a frivolous reply, but knowing it also held a hidden truth, jocularly answered: 'Because' – and here I quote his exact words – 'you're a finely tuned concatenation of carbon and water, and your main function is to keep your wife warm!'

It was tempting to laugh it off and to concede a well-earned debating point, but the doctor had a point. Physically we are no more than a combination of gasses, albeit a pretty sophisticated combination, but whatever meaning is to be given to our being, it will be determined in relation to another being or beings. Our individual identities are shaped by the identities of others, and the deeper we get into the Gospel of Thomas, the more we realise that identity is at its heart. It's an exploration of identity: Thomas' own identity, how his own self-understanding was bound up with the identity of Jesus, and of how far God could be identified with Jesus, and how Jesus conceived of God's identity.

Personhood has always held a particular fascination for Christians, to the extent that the early fathers could think of no other way to express the indefinable nature of God, and of our experience of the Divine, than as one God in three Persons, which is unintelligible were it not also to hold a kernel of truth. In the light of modern developments in neuroscience and psychology newer, harder questions have overtaken those of the early church fathers. Not only, who are we, but what are we?

> Jesus said, 'it seems you've not yet recognized me by what I say to you. Some of you are like people who claim loyalty to God without being interested in what God says, and some of you are like those who discuss what God says without being interested in God.' (GofTh 43b)

We may think we know ourselves better than anyone, even than our loved ones and our most intimate friends can know us, but we know too how we can be surprised and shocked by aspects of ourselves we never knew were there. And so it was for Thomas. He realised from some of the things Jesus had told them, as well as when he was watching Jesus, particularly when Jesus wasn't aware that he was being watched, that it had been like that for Jesus too: an unfolding of a messianic self or the delusions of a maverick?

> *The friends of Jesus said to him, 'We'd like to know who you really are. Where have you got your ideas from?'* (GofTh 43a)

The psychologist and the sociologist tell us that identity is 'a person's conception and expression of their individual or group affiliations', in other words, not just who we think we are, and who we know we are, but what do others know us for? Identity thus has a social as well as a personal dimension. We define ourselves over and against others. Matters of ethnicity and of gender take on a significant and sometimes sinister aspect when we fear our own self-understanding is in danger of being marginalised.

Changes in the law in Britain and other western states redefining marriage as same sex, as well as different sex, unions have challenged long held assumptions regarding the physical expression of love, and the nature of the family. It has confused the traditionalists, for whom the appearance matters more than honesty in shaping the identity of a wholesome society, and it has troubled many good folk within faith communities who have yet to reconcile how people are, with what they have been taught people should be. Moreover, the denial of the sexual identity of another can indicate a denial of the incertainties inherent in most sexuality. 'And God saw all that he had made, and it was very good.'[30]

Nationhood, and the recognition of different ethical strands within nationhood, is the other significant area in which identity is recognised, affirmed and too often fought over, with disastrous consequences. So there are regular debates in western societies over immigration and integration, and the results are seldom edifying. Tribal religion has succeeded too often in shouting down true religion that upholds the essence of faith to be the recognition of God in the other.

The former bishop of Rochester, Michael Nazir Ali, sees western identity as a whole currently under threat from what he identifies as the 'triple jeopardy' of 'aggressive secularism, radical Islam and multiculturalism'. His response is a kind of call to arms, a rallying cry to those who share his concerns, 'to work against the grain' of these influences.[31] No less aware of these trends, Rowan Williams, the former Archbishop of Canterbury, takes a more creative approach, defining the state's role 'as one of overseeing a variety of communities of religious convictions and, where necessary, assisting them to keep the peace together'.[32]

The ultimate unity of the whole of humankind is a deeply embedded yearning, however impossible it may seem. That it is there at all is an indication of an inherent recognition of an identity that transcends all our divisions, and taxes us with the ongoing task of allowing for a true inclusivity that affirms difference. And it has become an even more pressing ambition as we have become increasingly aware of our global inter-dependence and of the vulnerability of this shared earth.

I have never forgotten being asked by an elderly church member during a visit to East Germany before the collapse of the Berlin wall: 'Do they know about us in the west?' It expressed the awful loneliness that besets the human spirit when it fears its fears are no longer being recognised. The role of the church in an unnamed East European country is the theme of Irish author, Brian Moore's thriller, *The Colour of Blood*.[33] Preaching during Mass, the hero, Cardinal Bem, tells his congregation that they live under 'the tyranny of an age when religious beliefs have become inextricably entwined with political hatreds.' Such tyrannies did not pass away when the Berlin wall came down. They emerge in every society where religion is abused.

There was no getting away from the matter of identity in first-century Palestine. A forgotten people, subsumed into the all-encompassing empire that was Rome, despite everything that had been promised in the Torah: 'You will be to me a kingdom of priests, my holy nation.'[34] For Thomas it had looked as if Jesus had been the person to reclaim their identity, to restore their uniqueness, even though he seemed to show no animosity to Roman soldiers and their alien way of life.

Thomas was still some way from being convinced that the truth of identity lies in a recognition of the inherent incertainties attached to faith. But he knew himself well enough to know it had been coming to a head gradually ever since that last supper. He needed to see.

He remembered the time the authorities had pulled over a man who'd traded on being blind all his life, and apparently was now as able to get about like any other sighted person. He told them he'd had his sight back, but he'd no idea of the name of the healer. The authorities found out soon enough! Not wanting to make a fool of themselves, they even checked with the man's parents that he really had been blind from birth! Jesus might still have got away with it, but the trouble was the blind man insisted he'd been healed on Shabbat! Thomas thought Jesus deliberately went out of his way to annoy the authorities, as if he didn't care, or wanted to make a point. What point, though? 'And God said, let there be light.' Was that it?[35]

'There was once a man ...'

As Thomas wandered the streets of Jerusalem in a kind of post-crucifixion torpor, trying to figure out what had gone wrong, various incidents from their time together came back to him, to haunt and fascinate him afresh. In the cryptic, sometimes esoteric Sayings of Jesus, Thomas would come closest to fathoming the mystery of the rabbi's wisdom. But he couldn't also forget the stories with which Jesus seemed to hold huge crowds in raptures: parables about farmers and vindictive neighbours:

'A farmer sowed his seed, but during the night, someone who didn't like the farmer very much sowed weeds among the seed ...' (GofTh 57a)

Stories about speculators who got their priorities wrong:

'There was once a man who came into a large amount of money. He decided to build a farm...' (GofTh 63[i]a)

Tales of fair-minded employers and scheming tenants:

A landowner let out his property to tenant farmers who agreed to supply him with a proportion of the produce as rent. When he sent his agent to collect what was due to him, they grabbed hold of him, beat him up and very nearly killed him. When he reported to the landowner what had happened, the landowner said, 'Perhaps they didn't know who you were.' When he tried again with another agent, the same thing happened. The next time the landowner sent his son. He said, 'Perhaps they'll show a bit of respect for my son.' ... (GofTh 65[iii]a)

Thomas remembered how the crowd had once lost all sense of time as it listened to Jesus telling these pithy stories, and the people, too many to count – as many as five thousand some said – had been insistent on staying in case they missed a sequel.

Once, close to Passover, Jesus had turned the occasion into a kind of communal sacred meal. A youngster had put his own bread into the rabbi's hands: five barley loaves. And Jesus had blessed the bread. A couple of fish too. Fish: the first act of creation in the Torah. There'd been more than enough for everyone. Leftovers galore: twelve baskets full. That day we'd all been convinced Messiah had come. That we'd witnessed the beginning of a new creation. The crowds wanted to make

Jesus king, there and then. Now we knew better. Herod was king. Caesar was emperor. Anyway, not Jesus' style. Numbers again, thought Thomas: five thousand, twelve, five, two. What did it all add up to? Was it meant to add up to anything, anyway?[36]

In the numbing, desolate aftermath of the crucifixion, as Thomas chased his memories in and out of the holy city's alleys, pungent with the smell of Passover's butchered meat, he found himself reluctantly skirting the temple, its magnificent permanence seeming to mock the delusion of a crucified Messiah. Where was the meaning in what he and the rest of them had heard, seen, felt, touched? Clues? All they seemed to be given were clues. So many questions.

Not long after that sacred hillside meal, Thomas remembered how Jesus had gone off on his own for a bit. He did that quite often. A conversation with our Father was how he described it when we asked him afterwards where he'd been, what he'd been doing. Very close, Jesus and his Father. Taught us, too, to call God, Abba. More endearing than 'father', more intimate. Meantime, we'd taken a boat to the other side of the Sea of Galilee. Not a good idea. Failed to read the signs. Caught in a frightful storm. Thought our number was up, all of us. Then this voice, coming towards us over the water. And it was him! Telling us not to worry. That he could still the storm. Somehow or other we all got to land in one piece. But it had been uncanny, as if he'd been walking the waves, patting them down, calming the wind, so we'd be safe.[37]

3 When did Thomas crack?

Lord, we do not know where you are going, so how can we know the way?[38]

AT THE TIME the Passover lambs were being ritually slaughtered, Jesus would be hanging from a Roman cross. Before then, there was to be this last meal with his friends in an upper room in Jerusalem. An ordinary meal in an ordinary house that became extraordinary because of what was to follow and what was remembered.

It was the week before Passover, the annual Jewish festival, when Jews recalled their exodus tradition of deliverance from slavery and of their settlement in a promised land. Jesus, however, did not expect to celebrate this Passover. The carpenter's son from the backwoods of Nazareth had built up too formidable a following with his disturbing, liberating gospel. It had become a serious challenge to the careful, but uneasy balance between the two unequal administrations of Caesar and the Temple. In Luke's account, Jesus tells his friends as much at this their last supper together; he knows time is running out: 'never again shall I eat (Passover) until the time when it finds its fulfilment in the Kingdom of God'.[39]

There was bread on the table and wine in a pitcher. The long table with half a dozen male figures seated either side of the honoured guest is a conceit of the Renaissance. This was the unpretentious upstairs room of a Jewish family with everyone crowding in; children chattering, teasing, laughing, and the grownups doing what adults have always done at family gatherings: engaging in more than one conversation at once, often superficially, occasionally intently, predicting the imminent demise of the current occupation, and boasting to cover their unadmitted fears. And in the conviviality of this pre-Passover moment, there'd been the rabbi's thoughts to engage their hearts and minds.

In the haze of the meal and the sharpness of the moment, it dawned on Thomas that none of it made sense. 'We don't know where you're going.' All the stuff that had gone on before: weeks, months, years of it, travelling with the charismatic rabbi from Galilee, hoping he'd turn out to be 'Messiah', wanting him to be the promised one, willing the Day of the Lord. Suddenly none of it added up. It was just so much broken bread.

A post-Freudian age would diagnose a nervous breakdown at that ordinary meal that particular night, his life unravelling. It just hit him that he was slowly coming apart at the seams: sensible, cautious, vulnerable Thomas.

The feedback from the rabbi when the lamps were low and the lights were dim only accentuated the gulf between them at that moment: 'I am.' 'I am.' 'I am.' But Thomas had already lost it. And Thomas knew it. He was breaking up inside. The others just passed it off as Thomas being awkward again. But Thomas wasn't being awkward. Thomas was suffering. Thomas was hurting. Thomas was not waving.

In one obvious sense that was the moment Thomas cracked. But that would be a superficial assessment. This was the culmination of something that had been going on for a long time, gradually building up, layer upon layer of unease with so many unacknowledged incertainties. 'When' is rarely a moment. More often it is a long time coming, but when it does it's terrible in its destructive force. But it also contains within it the possibility of a transformative renewal.

In attempting to analyse this pivotal point in the story, it is necessary to ascertain its significance, not only for a better assessment of this elusive disciple and his startling Gospel, but also for its insight into a Jesus we thought we'd got the measure of from the four canonical gospels. In the process we will be able, maybe, to pick up resonances with our own ruptured times, which are also facing a kind of collective breakdown as some old certainties are questioned and the various religious systems that once offered a way through are found to be themselves in a state of crisis.

'You know where I'm going'

But to begin with the incident as it's set down in the Fourth Gospel.

It was the night before Jesus was arrested, though all but one of the disciples seemed uniformly unaware of the likelihood of such an outcome. The one who knew was the one who brought it about, Judas Iscariot, though his motives have never been satisfactorily explained.

Jesus had just said: 'There's plenty of room in God's house. I would have warned you otherwise. I'm going to make things ready for you. That means I'll come back to fetch you later. Then we shall all be together. You know where I'm going and how to get there, don't you?' To which Thomas objected, 'We've no idea where you're going, so how can we know how to get there?'[40]

The question is indicative of a tradition almost submerged in the later presentation of the story that at the core of the earliest Christian narrative there was a far greater willingness to engage with truth, a welcoming of the questioning of untested assumptions.

The friends of Jesus said to him, 'What will happen to us in the end?' (GofTh 18)
The friends of Jesus said to him, 'We never know when we're going to see you next.' (GofTh 37)

The Gospel of Thomas is important because it substantiates the significance of that tradition. Thomas is not a 'bit player' in the unfolding of the drama that grapples with the meaning of Jesus. Other friends of Jesus questioned things, but as the disciple who asked the ultimate questions, Thomas is made to assume a representative identity, whilst also giving permission for all genuine seekers since, not to be afraid to ask the big questions, the awkward questions, the uncomfortable questions, and to be prepared to live with the answers, however costly.

Judaism, the first and the original of the three great monotheistic faiths, is the one that historically is most able to handle incertainty. The ancient literature of the Torah and the Talmud reveals a religion never at ease with itself, which is a good basis for avoiding too much spurious certainty. For them God is to be argued with, not surrendered to unthinkingly. Their spirituality is an endless tussle with an almost tangible deity who is tantalisingly elusive and winsomely present in unexpected places and moments. Their history saves them from a facile faith.

Today's Jews might not talk much about their God, but their memories, their experiences, their awareness of the history of their people over successive millennia have made them wary of too much certainty. They are one generation on from the generation of the Shoah – the 'calamity' of the Nazi programme of systematic genocide that also targeted Gypsies and Gays, and any kind of awkward nonconformity. Jews like Rudi, who features in a beautiful collection of Life Portraits from a Jewish Community in Cardiff, published under the title,'Hineni' – 'Here I am'.[41]

Rudi was born in Berlin in 1924, the only child of a Romanian father and a British-born Jewish mother. 'Luckily my parents managed to get out of Germany on a Romanian passport,' he remembers. 'I think the force of my parents coming to England was my mother. She said, "either we go or we perish" ...' In Yehuda Amichai's haunting verse, Jews know from bitter personal experience the dangers of 'The Place Where We Are Right', that – 'From the place where we are right/Flowers will never grow/In the spring.' They know how: '... doubts and loves/Dig up the world/Like a mole, a plough.'[42]

A portrait of his father's grandmother hangs framed on the wall of Rudi's living room. 'When my father fled Romania,' Rudi explains, 'he took a passport photo of her with him to Berlin, and when he was able to afford it he had it enlarged and then painted.' It's a dark image that testifies to a hard life, but for Rudi, it 'is like the Mona Lisa – beyond value'. And in his Reform Synagogue, where his wife, Herta, is commemorated in stained-glass, he refers proudly to a pair of candlesticks that came originally from their home in Berlin. Out of such threads is faith woven and sustained. Rudi Montrose died in 2010, aged 85, one of the last survivors of a generation of Jews for whom certainty's inheritance had spelled angst, and hope been born of incertainty.

Christianity is less at ease over the unavoidable tension between certainty and incertainty. Its insights have led it to a conviction that God's essential characteristics, as far as the human mind can grasp, are both finite and infinite, within time and outside time. Because what else is the doctrine of the Trinity but a picture of God who is infinite, being seen and revealed in a moment in time as human, to be experienced 'in the spirit' ever after. An impossible to pin down God, but always exciting, revealed in suffering, redeeming in love:

Other people won't understand you until you understand yourself.
(GofTh 3b)

Christianity struggles incessantly, inconclusively, as it must, not only to keep up with its insights into God, but to earth its interpretation and expression of those insights in terms of a particular understanding of the certainty of the unfathomable nature of God. It struggles with its willingness to acknowledge the importance of incertainty in its interpretation of its beliefs, because, if God not only exists but is at least as Christians believe God to be, then our minds and our hearts can never risk being closed to the unfathomable, and the interpretation must always be provisional.

A forensic computer consultant once described to me how he and his wife had 'occasionally discussed and explored the various phenomena observable in the universe, and also the dimensions of it, and some related issues, only to arrive at a point, 'where there is a question to which the only correct answer, currently, is "No one knows".' An avowed agnostic, he went on to admit: 'The gospels very cleverly and knowledgeably deal with people like me in the shape of St Thomas.'

In the Christian tradition Thomas, therefore, emerges as the carrier of the questions that trouble and that still haunt the genuine enquirer. There is no other character within the New Testament writings who is shown to be grappling with incertainty to the same extent, and grappling with it as an insider, as an apostle in the making, not as a marginal or disillusioned follower.

At the last supper it was Thomas who put his hand up to interrupt the flow of the rabbi's sophisticated farewell discourses, five chapters long, with a show-stopper of a question: 'How can we know?' The certainties that had kept him together had begun to unravel. He had 'lost it'. There at the last supper, as Jesus broke bread the words and the actions collided, leading Thomas to feel exposed, dysfunctional, vulnerable.

Earlier Simon Peter had asked, 'Where are you going?'[43] But Thomas' enquiry is much more incisive, much more personal. The emphasis in Thomas' question is on the 'How?' of faith. 'How can I, we, get to the place of enlightenment, to God's Bright New World?'

'We don't know!' Thomas interrupts. 'We don't know! How can we ... can we ... can ...?'

The question in one form or another still perplexes and troubles those who are in earnest in their endeavour to nurture their spirituality, but unwilling, or, perhaps truer, unable, as creatures of a post-modern world, to handle the elusiveness of the intangible. 'We've no idea where you're going, so how can we know how to get there?'[44]

The question has a long pedigree. It's woven into the cloth of faith from the day it left the loom. It's a fine thread, from a refined skein. It's what gives belief the subtle complexity that strident Christianity has too often underplayed and under-valued.

In her one and only novel, the American poet, Sylvia Plath, describes the slow disintegration of her heroine, Esther, as madness takes over her ordered life. It's a barely disguised version of her own story. But it's also a parable of a collective madness that can overtake a whole culture when the incer-tainties become intolerable and there is no big narrative to help it find its way back to sanity. She remembers how, 'piece by piece, I fed my wardrobe to the night wind, and fleetingly, like a loved one's ashes, the grey scraps were ferried off, to settle here, there, exactly where I would never know in the dark heart of New York.'[45]

'Experienced that emptiness'

Thomas' 'breakdown' echoes this modern frustration with the incomprehensibility with which Christianity seems to wrap itself up too easily. 'We've no idea where you're going. What it's about? We sense, though, that without it we might be losing something rather important ...'

> Jesus said, 'Trust your senses! If you're honest at heart, your honesty will help you to understand everything in the world, in the way a strong light shows everything more clearly. If you're confused inside, then everything you see will be blurred.' (GofTh 24)

There's also something of the: 'there you go again' complaint in Thomas' response: a 'Why not cut the God-talk and get to the values' rejoinder. It's a very real problem for many. Can they bypass the theological package, the divinity module; can they live it without the myth? Maybe the myth is the icing on the cake for those with a sweet tooth? What happens, though, if you think the myth is the yeast that makes the whole thing rise? 'How can we know?' It's the 21st century's 'Scream'.[46] 'To the person in the bell jar and stopped as a dead baby,' Plath wrote, 'the world itself is a bad dream.'[47]

More recently none have captured the mood of Western despondency and despair more elegantly and intensely than Cormac McCarthy in his post-apocalyptic novel, *The Road*. 'There is no God,' the father tells his son in the barren landscape of their dogged trek to escape the enveloping cloud, 'and we are his prophets.'[48]

The 18th century's Enlightenment unseated the certainties of religion, but the latent ideas encapsulated by Christianity still continue to exercise a powerful hold, and to mould our social development, more than we sometimes realise or are willing to acknowledge. And perhaps the most disturbing idea of all is the one centred on the Palestinian Jew, called Jesus of Nazareth: Jesus the Christ.

Christianity can appear to be a very perplexing faith because it focuses on a figure in time, not for the religious genius of his teaching (though that is no small matter), but because of who he is held to have been by his human companions, then and since. God with us. It's over the top. It's an 'unnatural' faith.

Why the hold of such an uncomfortably illogical myth on so many minds and hearts for so long, and for millions still today? – Myth, in the sense of a story that hides a profound and abiding truth.

Does it matter if we let go of the myth's central idea, ditch it, subordinate it, relegate it? There's enough, more than enough in the treasure chest of the Nazarene's remembered words, and his remarkable stories. The force of his personality, even transmitted over such a distance of time, puts him up there with the religious greats of all time: Moses, the Buddha, Mohammed. Jesus was a reforming pioneer of exceptional character and persistence.

Why the hold on the imagination of so many for so long of an incarnated God who was as human as you or I? It doesn't make sense in any sense that can be called sensible. Or has the Judaeo-Christian myth hit on an insight that doesn't negate the other great faiths, but is also peculiar in the sense of being different in kind, if not in intention.

Even if many can't buy the Christian story exactly as it has been filtered through centuries of preaching and teaching, can they, nevertheless, buy into the myth as a meeting point between the imagined and the real?

'Is there anything there?' The question is as old as the old, old story; the question is often presented as a religious one, but it is also indicative of the western post-modern loss of direction. We are beset by fears for the future of our planet. We worry that our capitalist economy might be awry in some fundamental way, and with every bank that collapses, with every currency that falters, and with every alarm over a temporary glitch in the performance of a particular Automated Teller Machine we panic. 'Is there anything there?', therefore, becomes a question that challenges the very values of our way of life.

Jesus said, 'You must get to know all about the world in order to discover how empty it is.' (GofTh 56)

The Gospel of Thomas implies a far less cut and dried religious tradition than church teaching has sometimes assumed, and is much more encouraging of the notion of incertainty as better able to penetrate the mystery of our own existence and the being of God, than any number of so-called certainties.

When the poet-playwright Saunders Lewis,[49] a convert Catholic from a Presbyterian background, looked for a vehicle for a post-war play on the nature of tradition, the perils of love and the limits of science, he turned to the myth of Blodeuwedd from the medieval cycle of Celtic tales, the Mabinogion.[50]

As with all the great fables of the world, there are morals nestling in the magic, and spirituality is often affirmed through myth. For Lewis, the science that could magic a split atom into a mushroom cloud was dangerous alchemy divorced from spiritual awareness. Infidelity to the values of the past had also left human kind vulnerable and disoriented. There were memories that needed to be restored and redeemed. Is it reading too much into the play to wonder whether in the myth of a slain eagle being resurrected in human form Lewis also saw a Christian parallel?

'How can we know?'

Ours is an age that rightly recoils from those who would impose on others ideas and interpretations based on literal readings of ancient writings; that fears the fundamentalism that diminishes the intellect, that crinkles up the soul and fails to restrain the imagination from playing conjuring tricks with reality. Ours is an age that rejects attempts to suppress an honest engagement with uncomfortable questions. People today respect more the modesty of those who uncover the mysteries of the universe, impressed by their rejection of certainty in the restless quest for knowledge. But we are also uncomfortable with limitless incertainty.

In this exasperatingly narrow corridor between incertainty and certainty institutional religion has blundered and stumbled too often. It has wanted to sound certain, but about the wrong things, about matters where incertainty would have been the better course.

It wasn't until the second millennium was drawing to an end that the Roman Catholic Church finally and formally retracted its condemnation of Galileo for asserting that the earth orbited around the Sun! The inquisition had condemned him because his observations did not square with its reading of scripture or the church's official teaching. In reversing that earlier decision in 1993, Pope John Paul II[51] described Galileo as a victim of 'tragic mutual incomprehension' – though it was actually the Papacy that was uncomprehending!

'It would seem that parts of the Church in general have not learned much from this error,' my church-going father-in-law remarked at the time, 'for how many other victims have there been, of this "tragic mutual incomprehension"? Abolition of the slave trade had to contend with justification of this evil practice by clerics who appealed to the Bible for support. Darwin was roundly condemned by church leaders and, in our own time, the Church in South Africa, until recently, had lent its support to apartheid.'

He was quite right, of course. Institutions committed to the exploration of spirituality as an 'experience of God and the trans-formation of lives as the outcome of that experience'[52] have faltered when experience collided with incertainty. In Brecht's play, A Life of Galileo, the astronomer concludes, 'Where faith sat for thousands of years, there now sits doubt. All the world says: Yes we know what's written in the books but now let's see what our eyes tell us.'[53]

Jesus said, 'Unless you escape from the patterns of thought and conduct given you by your parents, unless you develop your own personality, distinct from your brothers and sisters, as I've done, you won't be fit to be a member of my team.' (GofTh 55)

There has been too much trading in self-important certainties to the neglect of the realities with which religion should be concerned, because religion – all religions – have been guilty too often of being certain about the wrong things! And uncertain in those areas where religion should have believed it had something unique to contribute, a distinctive angle to offer, not on 'what our eyes tell us', but on how to measure 'what our eyes tell us' against our other senses.

Religion has been woefully hesitant about those areas and insights within its competence and experience that it should have contributed to the public discourse with far greater confidence. Thomas needed to know. If he was to go, if the rest of them were to go, wherever the rabbi was going, then they needed to know.

Jesus said, 'I'm going to bring about a revolution which no one can reverse!' (GofTh 71)

We all need to know, but only so much perhaps as we can live with at the time. It's not so much the withholding of the truth as the realisation that the truth is only progressively grasped. The process of our spiritual refinement is a gradual one; it is an accumulation of insights that allow us to see a bit more, or to see the same thing differently or more of the same more clearly. The fundamentalist finds changing perspectives scary, and so risks never needing to know more. The innate curiosity that enables us to become fuller, more rounded human beings is lost, and each new insight threatens to dismantle the whole precarious edifice, rather than providing the opportunity to come at it anew and to discover its inexhaustible potential to surprise.

It was said of the award-winning American journalist and poet Eliza Griswold, that despite her deeply Christian upbringing, she gradually lost the certainty of Christianity's exclusive absolute truths in favour of a 'cloud of ambiguity in which most people live.'[54] But ambiguity and faith are not mutually exclusive.

Thomas needed to know, but he was learning slowly that it wasn't a once and for all knowing, but a progressive knowing, each new bit of knowing making him question the last knowing and all the time growing in understanding of himself and of the divine.

'How can we know?' Thomas asked. And the answer he got

was: 'I am'.

Jesus said, 'You can see what someone looks like on the outside, but their relationship to God is hidden and mysterious.' (GofTh 83)

When Charles Dickens wrote his great death bed scene for young Paul in his novel, *Dombey and Son*, he portrayed the boy as already seeing into the next life, and in particular already recognising the face of the eternal, resurrected Jesus waiting to welcome him. With his last breath, Dickens portrays the boy directing his sister to, 'tell them that the print upon the stairs at school is not divine enough. The light about the head is shining as I go.' I have written elsewhere how an earlier age would not have found that scene either embarrassing or sentimental. It affirmed a certainty that many today are uncomfortable with: a cultural certainty that we just do not have.[55]

Had Dickens been writing today, however, I imagine that he might well have had the boy say: 'tell them that the print above the stairs at school is not human enough'. Rather than being dazzled by haloes, we are much more likely to take someone seriously who shows us the potential of our humanity to express divinity.

'A hole in the bottom of the bag'

The exchange between Thomas and Jesus in that upstairs room one night in Jerusalem long ago, moreover, is not only significant for what it reveals about discipleship, but more so for what it reveals about Jesus, the rabbi from Nazareth. The discovery of Thomas' Gospel has challenged our certainties about who he was, and how he taught, and why we need a new language to explain him, and his revelation of God, to a less godly age.

The teenager who dug up the pot near Nag Hammadi one December day in 1945, in which the Gospel of Thomas had survived the ravages of time, could have had no inkling that its contents would end up causing furrows of enquiry leading to some radical rethinking about the preaching and teaching techniques of the very founder of Christianity.

The codex that turned out to be the Gospel of Thomas captures a style, even in translation, that has more of an authentic Aramaic feel, than we're used to from the texts of the New Testament as we have them. Even more remarkably, it implies that the Teacher's favoured teaching method was closer to what we might think of as riddles: sayings phrased in a way that is not immediately easy to understand, but which those who heard them could never forget.

> *Jesus said, 'You're very sharp in your observation of the world of nature, but you've not observed me very closely. You're not even aware of the challenge I'm giving you this very moment.'* (GofTh 91b)

What the Gospel of Thomas does, therefore, is not so much to show us a different Jesus from the one we've become familiar with in the canonical Gospels, but to change the way we read and hear those Gospels, and see the Jesus to whom they witness. It shows us a Jesus who was not only comfortable with fielding questions from friends and foes alike, but with a style that also encouraged his enquirers never to be satisfied with pat answers. For Jesus, insight was not something you learned, but something you discovered, as you grappled with life's incertainties.

> *Jesus said to his friends, "How would you describe me, as compared with other people?"*
> *Peter said, "You're like a reporter who gets the facts right."*
> *Matthew said, "You're a deep thinker who makes good sense."*
> *Thomas said, "Teacher, I'm lost for words!"*
> *Jesus said, "I'm not your teacher. I'm just somebody standing by the spring of knowledge, inviting people to drink."* (GofT 13a)

In this, and many other Sayings from the Gospel of Thomas, what becomes clear is that Jesus' language, his way of teaching is thoroughly Semitic. It was only as his story came to be shared with a wider Greek and Latin world that it began to lose its Semitic edge. In the process, something of the startling rawness of the original was sacrificed, its impact muted, Latinised, distanced.

Modern readers have become so accustomed to the mellifluous reasonableness of the prose of the canonical Gospels that they tend to hear the preaching and teaching of Jesus as the pronouncements of some classical rhetorician! It's a shock, therefore, to find him, for instance, saying:

'If, like me, you know your Mum and Dad, then, like me, they'll call you a bastard!' (GofTh 105)

Scholars have always been aware of a missing link between Jesus' original voice and his voice as recorded in the canonical Gospel accounts. The discovery of the Gospel of Thomas proved to be a revelation. Even in the Coptic, in which it survived, the Gospel of Thomas reads more like a translation of an original Aramaic text. The language of the Gospel of Thomas may be that missing link. It may be that this Gospel reflects more truly the language in which Jesus taught and preached and told stories, than the narrative works of the canonical evangelists.

The sonorous and much loved language of the 1611 King James version of the Bible has further lulled an English speaking world into thinking that what we are reading, what we are hearing is as close to the rhythms and style of the first-century Jesus as we can expect at this distance of time and in translation. The discovery of the Gospel of Thomas allows us a different, fresher way of accessing the mind of the Master, with a message that could crack and mend. With its discovery, we may be better able to find a Jesus who is both much more challenging and a lot more surprising.

The so-called crisis of faith besetting Christianity, in particular, is an inability to reinterpret itself in such a way that it connects with a modern understanding of life, without losing its audacious insight as to why 'that little piece of human history called "Jesus of Nazareth" holds the key to the nature of God and of human destiny.' [56]

In Islam it is a book, rather than a person who holds the key to faith. Its Sufi sect, however, succeeds in making a distant deity personally present, transforming Allah's assurance, 'We created man – We know what his soul whispers to him: We are closer to him than his jugular vein'[57], into a living encounter. 'Sell your cleverness,' said the Sufi poet Rumi, 'and buy bewilderment.'[58] Issues of certainty and incertainty are bypassed in the ecstasy of losing oneself in the being of God. 'God reveals himself in the heart of the mystic, while remaining one and transcendent ... The mystic's ego encounters God through love and is ultimately consumed in the unity of God.'[59]

On his journey through Arabia, the travel writer, Jonathan Raban was told, 'you hardly ever meet an Arab who's an unbeliever. He may take a drink or two, of course, and go around in London in a suit, and meet you down at the Flying Boat – but he never even begins to think of himself as not being a Muslim. ... They don't make a great palaver about Doubt, like Christians do.'[60]

In the other great world faiths, certainty, in an either/or, academic sense, would appear to be less of an issue than it is for the monotheistic religions, with Buddhism (as a philosophy rather than a religion) following a different path towards enlightenment. For Zen the question is not, How can we know? but 'why stop or go round or go back – why not go over?' Buddhism is about pushing the boundaries, not in a right or wrong sense, but in exploring the limits of human compassion and reverence for life.

For the Hindu, similarly, discipleship is following a particular path, perfecting a particular lifestyle, nurturing contemplation, rather than challenging the intellectual validity of its scriptures, the Vedas. 'Life and death, joy and sorrow, gain and loss,' it teaches, 'These dualities cannot be avoided. Learn to accept what you cannot change.'[61]

Differences of perception and insight into the nature and being of God on this scale are an obvious challenge to establishing common ground between the different faiths. But if we give up on the search we can expect little prospect of creative international harmony or of cooperation on major global and environmental issues. The challenge is immense, and goes way beyond the ecumenism of inter-church dialogue. This is 'twinning' on an inter-religious scale, and it cannot be avoided if we are to reach a stage where a person's belief becomes part of the solution rather than part of the problem.

Jesus said, 'You'll be truly human when you learn to live in harmony. Then you'll overcome all obstacles.' (GofTh 106)

For Christians that means coming to terms with the fact that incertainties have been far more integral to their story than they have been prepared to acknowledge in the past. That's why the Fourth Gospel highlights the incertainties of Thomas. They are integral to the tradition. Otherwise, why attribute to one of the surviving witnesses to the events surrounding the life and teaching of the crucified rabbi, questions that imply an element of Apostolic incertainty, if not that incertainty was an essential element of early Christianity and of how Jesus taught his followers? There's an elusive, fragile quality to the Kingdom of God, to God's New World, that we endanger when we are over-zealous for a certainty faith will not allow.

Jesus said, 'God's New World is like someone walking from the shop with a bag of flour. They haven't noticed there's a big hole in the bottom of the bag, and they leave a long trail of wasted flour behind them. Imagine how they feel when they get home!' (GofTh 97)

Over the centuries the churches have been over zealous in promoting and preserving the certainties of the faith, paying insufficient attention to the mysteries of the faith. Thomas thus becomes the agent for asking the big question, the God question.

We don't know where you are going, so how can we know the way? It's almost childlike in its intensity. 'I don't want to lose you, but how can I not in the midst of so much uncertainty?' The question is in the record because it's the key to understanding the nature of faith and of the limitations of the human quest for credible certainties. One of the best things about going to church for the winsome, vulnerable African child, Cherish Arkolo in Michael Arditti's novel, *Easter*,[62] is 'making pictures of the angels who fly round the ceiling on wings that beat as fast as a headache before a pill. And although no human person can see them, they're not invisible', she explains. 'They're like whistles that can only be heard by dogs. So church is the one place where having eyes is no help, since everyone is as blind as her.'

It's because 'church', all the churches, especially the historic churches, have been uncomfortable with the incertainties of faith, that many genuine seekers have been left stranded and disillu-sioned. 'We face a cultural landscape of need,' says church historian and British ecumenist David Cornick, 'a landscape that seems almost in a spiritual infancy, longing for the God it dare no longer name.'[63]

'If I tried to tell you'

There is one remaining 'twinning' conundrum to be unravelled, however, before we need to dig even further back to unlock why Thomas cracked at Jesus' last supper before his crucifixion, and it is to do with the relationship between the Gospel of Thomas, and the Fourth Gospel.

'How can we know?' Thomas asks in the Fourth Gospel. 'How can we know?'

What an audacious question to throw at God!

It was addressed to Jesus, of course, but given that it's in the Fourth Gospel, we're intended to understand that it was really addressed to God. That's what the Fourth Gospel does. It plays on your mind. It's like a swathe of shot silk or a bale of changeable taffeta. The colour of the warp is shot through with the tint of the weft. It depends on the angle of the light and on how you hold it, wear it, feel it, which shade you see shimmering in the folds.

The question was addressed to Jesus but it was also addressed to God. This teasing, tantalising, troublesome Fourth Gospel seems to want it both ways, and to want us to see that we can't begin to fathom the one without the other. That we cannot really, truly understand our own humanity without an awareness of our divine potential, of our latent capacity to become: 'little less than a god'.[64] That we cannot understand God if we do not at least entertain the wild, wounding, worshipful thought, even if we do not, cannot ever wholly assimilate it, that God can be known, if ever God can be known, in the shape and the feel of flesh and blood, of brain and bone, in human skin and sinew.

Before the Gospel of Thomas was recently discovered, all we knew of Thomas was from what we could piece together from the four interventions he'd been credited with in the Fourth Gospel. Nothing in Matthew, Mark or Luke, only his name: Thomas, Didymus, The Twin. Why is Thomas only fleshed out in the Fourth Gospel? Why is he only quoted there? Thomas' interventions seem sufficiently significant to warrant their inclusion in all their versions too. But we search those three gospels in vain to hear the voice of Thomas.

Might the answer have something to do with a common thread running through both the Gospel of Thomas and the

Fourth Gospel, sharing a twinned spirituality whilst retaining distinctive and separate identities? Might both be the product of a particular household of faith, intent on getting at the truth behind the events of which they'd been a part? Might they have both been nurtured in an environment where they were encouraged to ponder the question of what it might mean if divinity and humanity were once to collide?

In his introduction to *Good as New*, John Henson speculates on the authorship of the Fourth Gospel originating in just such a community, namely the one based at Bethany, in the home of Mary, Martha and their brother Lazarus, whom he also identifies as the unnamed 'beloved disciple' at the last supper.

This, of course, runs counter to the long tradition that the Fourth Gospel was the work of the Galilean fisherman, the apostle John, later referred to as John of Ephesus, of whom the second-century bishop of Alexandria, Clement, noted that 'last of all', after Matthew, Mark and Luke, 'John, perceiving that the external facts had been made plain in the Gospel, being urged by his friends, and inspired by the Spirit, composed a spiritual Gospel.'[65] There is also a non-Biblical tradition that this is the same John who brought Mary, the mother of Jesus, to end her days in Ephesus.

But how reliable is any of this tradition? Ephesus, on the western coast of modern-day Turkey, is much more closely identified with the apostle Paul than it is with the fisherman disciple, John. Whatever part Ephesus eventually played in the final coming together of the Fourth Gospel, Henson's theory that it began its life as the product of a community based in and around Bethany certainly has its attraction.

A common origin for The Fourth Gospel and the Gospel of Thomas would also account, not only for Thomas being quoted exclusively in the Fourth Gospel, whereas he's just a name in a list in the other three, but more to the similarity in themes between the two, especially of the significance of light. In the

Gospel of Thomas, for instance, Jesus says:

> *'I'm the light shining everywhere. I'm the sum total of everything.'*
> (GofTh 77a)

– and in the Fourth Gospel: 'I am the light of the world. No follower of mine shall walk in darkness; he shall have the light of life.'[66]

In the Gospel of Thomas, Jesus says:

> *'… a strong light shows everything more clearly. If you're confused inside, everything you see will be blurred.'* (GofTh 24)

– and in the Fourth Gospel: 'Trust to the light while you have it, so that you may become children of light.'[67]

'How can we know?' Thomas had asked at the last supper. And the answer he was given was: 'I am'. And he knew, as his people had been taught from the time of Moses onwards, that 'I am' was the name by which God had chosen to be known. 'Jesus replied, "I am the way, the truth and the life."' But is it as simple as that?

> *Jesus said … 'If you have open and inquisitive minds, you'll get the answers you're looking for.'* (GofTh 92a)

It's another of those riddles: God is the way, as God is truth and light. But Jesus may be saying more, implying more. Maybe?

Might, therefore, Jesus' reply to Thomas, namely, 'I am the way, the truth and the life', carry a double meaning? It's about God. But is Jesus saying it's also about him? It's playing with ideas of humanity and divinity. God becomes human, so that humanity may become divine. Is that not what the 'no one comes to the Father but by me', after 'I am the way, the truth and the life', means? You, Thomas, and every other Thomas, male and female, have it in you to become divine.

The fourth-century bishop of Alexandria – the same Athanasius who'd clamped down on Gnostic unorthodoxy – could himself sound quite controversial with his insistence that God became human in order that humanity might become divine. It's an emphasis that is still characteristic of eastern Christianity. The churches of the East, as opposed to the Western church, which was more influenced by rational, Latin interpretations, seem to be more in touch with Christianity's Hebrew origins. The East was, and is, more comfortable with mystery. It is not disturbed by the mist that reveals as much as it obscures. It senses that the mystery and miracle of our humanity is hidden in incertainty. Byzantine theology is, therefore, not afraid to portray God using icons.

After the incident in which Jesus asked his followers, 'How would you describe me, as compared to other people?' and Thomas had been rebuked and taken to one side for addressing Jesus as 'Teacher', we read that:

> When [Thomas] joined the other disciples again they said, "What did he say to you?" Thomas said, "If I tried to tell you, you'd kill me, and then you'd be in right trouble!" (GofTh 13c)

Why such an extreme reaction to whatever had transpired between him and Jesus, unless it implies that Thomas had sensed something in Jesus that the others had missed, something so outrageous, so confusing, that had Thomas voiced it, he'd have been accused of blasphemy? It was holding onto that secret that became the intolerable burden.

It's no bad thing to crack, to admit the difficulties, because only in that way will we be able to reconstruct ourselves to hold a more robust, authentic faith. One that doesn't deny the incertainties, but that somehow finds them reassuring rather than disturbing, because they save us from the delusion of believing that we've got it taped, got God taped, got Jesus taped:

'I'm not your teacher. I'm just somebody standing by the spring of knowledge, inviting people to drink.' (GofTh 13c)

A verse in Geoffrey Ainger's hymn, *Born in the night*, might have been written for Thomas: 'Truth of our life, Mary's child,/you tell us God is good:/prove it is true, Mary's child./Go to your cross of wood.'

4 Where was Thomas going?

'Let us also go and die with him.'[68]

THOMAS HAD COME to think of the family in Bethany as much
as his own friends as they were of Jesus. Languid Lazarus, who'd
never been in the best of health, but with a refined mind and a
particular interest in Hellenistic ideas. Mary, his sister, gifted
with deep spiritual intuition, and as much a disciple of Jesus as
any of those traditionally thought of as limited to the twelve.
And Martha, his other sister, who was more traditional in her
understanding of the place of women, though no less profound
than her siblings. She too could sometimes reveal an unexpected
streak of insight that took those who didn't know her well
completely by surprise.

When Jesus received an urgent message from these friends, it
concerned Thomas too. Mary and Martha had sent to say their
brother was seriously ill. If Jesus came at once, the implication
and the expectation was that Lazarus might well recover. But
Jesus delayed inexplicably, and it is possible to trace the
emergence of Thomas' crisis of faith from this time. For Thomas,
everything that followed proved to be an outworking of that
unasked question, Why the delay? It seemed as if Jesus had
deliberately ignored the sisters' cry for help, with the rabbi's
itinerant life in the northern territory going on much as before:
telling parables, touching the sick, and issuing the starling news
that the long expected Day of the Lord was imminent.

Then, when it was apparently too late to do anything about it,
Jesus told his disciples, not only that he knew Lazarus was dead,
but that it was time to act on it! It was as if he wanted them to
understand that he saw it as the sign he'd been waiting for. And
the only one of the disciples to react to what they'd heard was
Thomas.

They were to move sixty miles south, not to visit, but to stay, with the implication that things were coming to a head in Jesus' mind and that the final engagement would have to be at the very heart of their history as a chosen people: Jerusalem itself.

Earlier visits to Jerusalem had shown that whatever appeal Jesus might have among the crowds, the authorities regarded him as a destabilizing element in their delicate relationship with the occupying Romans. The primary aim of the ruling Sadducees was always to avoid everything and anything that would jeopardise the tradition. They saw their calling as upholding the Temple and its rituals until the Day of the Lord, when they expected their diligence and foresight to be rewarded and Messiah revealed.

What Thomas said at this critical moment in the development of the story of Jesus reveals all the ambiguity with which Thomas is associated, but more than that, it exposes faith's raw struggle. If the last supper was the moment when Thomas' crisis of faith finally boiled over, we can trace the first simmering of his engagement with faith's incertainties in his response to what he was reading into what Jesus had just told them. It was one thing for Jesus to go south to console his dead friend's grieving sisters, it was a very different matter to go south in order to take on the temporal principalities and powers.

Thomas' surprising, enigmatic, difficult to interpret response to Jesus' decision to go to Judea, now that Lazarus had died was a forceful: 'Let us also go and die with him'! Was that with Lazarus? Or with Jesus? The *Good as New* paraphrase doesn't pull its punches. It translates Thomas' interjection starkly: 'Come on, let's go. We'll probably end up dead' – like Lazarus! Either way, it's clear that Thomas knows, as the other disciples must know, that the move is motivated by more than a pastoral call on a bereaved and much loved family. This change of direction is about something more, it's about the initiation of a process that will probably end in death – all their deaths.

So the issues raised by Jesus' puzzling delay in not going to Bethany earlier, when Lazarus was still alive and when, presumably, Jesus could have healed him as he'd healed so many others, had made Thomas confront his inherent incertainties. But they'd also done something else: they'd revealed Thomas' unexpected tenacity.

'Conflict, killings, and all-out war'

'Let us go and die with him' is capable of being interpreted in a number of ways, as we shall discover, but the most obvious is its acceptance of what a later age would term 'the cost of discipleship'. Thomas was willing to suffer for and alongside Jesus, if that was what was required, and he urged the other disciples to do the same, because such is the strength of the 'us' in 'let us also go'.

Jesus said, 'I select my friends very carefully. I expect them to stand shoulder to shoulder with one another.' (GofTh 23)

As such, Thomas' 'Let us also go and die with him' has an ominously contemporary ring to it, as I discovered when I heard what had happened to a Syrian community in the foothills of Maaloula, some twenty miles north-east of Damascus, that I'd visited a few years previously.

I can still remember the moment when, with a group of ecumenical representatives, I first heard a Syrian Orthodox priest intone the Lord's Prayer in Western Aramaic, Jesus' mother tongue, handed down from one generation to another and still spoken in those parts. And the phrase from the prayer that Jesus had taught Thomas and all the disciples to pray, that strikes me most now, is the one about not bringing us to the time of trial; about being delivered from evil: 'Oo'la te-ellan l'niss-yoona.'

For the best part of two thousand years Maaloula's isolation, nestled in a crag in an overhanging mass of yellow-gold rock, had felt isolated enough to be overlooked as successive waves of invasion and political unrest swept around and through the region that had cradled Western Civilization. Then in the second decade of the third millennium, Maaloula found its isolation was no protection against Islamist bandits and extremists that threatened to displace an earlier peaceful co-existence between those who call God Allah and those who call God Abba.

Jesus said, ... 'Disgraceful are those born with tender human qualities who choose to develop the behaviour of a wild animal.' (GofTh 7b)

Above the Monastery of Mar Takla – the holiest and oldest of Syria's Christian sites, dedicated to the legendary daughter of a Seleucid prince and a young disciple of Paul the Apostle, the domed church promised refuge, its sacred spring offered healing to a constant flow of Christian and Muslim pilgrims, in an easy acceptance of their common ancestry as the children of Abraham.

Presiding over the Monastery's dozen nuns and its orphanage for children from Christian families from all over the Middle East, was the redoubtable mother superior, Pelagia Sayaf. Foreign guests would always be received graciously and generously, worthy of the saint believed to have been buried there. But since the civil war, where the West was seen as arming Islamic fundamentalists against the secular Assad regime, they say the welcome became more muted.

As Mother Pelagia knelt in the great domed chapel, and contemplated the life of their patron saint, did the prediction of Jesus ring in her ears with an awful relevance:

Some people think I'll get the peoples of the world to live together in peace in no time at all. It's not as easy as that. What I have to say will lead to deep divisions, conflict, killings, and all-out war. Families will be torn apart, and individual members made to feel lonely and isolated. [GofTh 16]

I used to have a framed photograph on the wall of my study of a group of UK visitors to Syria, seven of us: a Roman Catholic bishop, a nurse (the only woman in the group), an Anglican priest, four Free Church ministers, together with a local Greek Orthodox bishop to prime and shepherd us. The party should also have included a Member of the European Parliament, but her visa application had been turned down.

I say I used to have, because I took it down recently It pained me to look at it, because the photo showed me with Bashar al-Assad in the People's Palace, in the Qassioun mountains overlooking Damascus from the north, and was a sad reminder of hopes for a better future for Syria, back in 2006.

Despite arriving in four official limousines along a route lined by armed soldiers, the sirens of the motorcyclist outriders blaring as we cut our way upwards through the morning rush hour traffic, the meeting itself had a beguiling intimacy, with only a couple of secretaries in attendance and a TV crew to capture the moment for the midday news bulletins, and a photographer to supply images for the next day's morning editions. After soft drinks, baklava and caramelised dates, the scene was set for serious discussion. What followed was a remarkably civilised and open exchange covering inter-faith relations, education, programmes to tackle poverty, prioritising research and development, responding to terrorism.

The United States, under President George W Bush, had broken off diplomatic relations with Syria, and the UK had followed suit, so a visit from a delegation from the west, however insignificant, was worth a lot of publicity. It showed there were people in the west at that time willing to give Syria the benefit of the doubt, until and unless proved otherwise. Apparently we were the only western church delegation ever to have had such a meeting. Our significance, however, did not even register on the Richter scale of the UK media, but in Syria the group not only made headline news but provided generous nightly footage for their national TV station, topped by a studio discussion recorded for subsequent transmission.

The UK Foreign Secretary at the time was the Rt Hon Jack Straw. The group sent him an open letter afterwards expressing its impression that al-Assad seemed to be 'committed to a process of change' and should therefore be offered qualified encouragement at least, if only to develop trade and cultural links between our two countries and to broker private sector support in new and innovative ways. We took it as a sign of al-Assad's more liberal reformist credentials that while we were there he'd appointed a woman as the second of his two Vice-Presidents, Najah al-Attar, a veteran literary academic, and we later had a meeting with a woman member of his cabinet, Bouthania Shaaban, Minister for Expatriates, who'd studied in the UK and had a doctorate on the relationship of the poetry of Shelley and the Chartists. And of course, Bashar himself had pursued a postgraduate course in ophthalmology in a London eye hospital, and had married a British Syrian, but his time away from Syria had only been eighteen months, and for all his fluency in English and his easy manner, he was probably more his father's son than we wanted to believe, and why it took the world so long to acknowledge it.

It is easy with hindsight to say the group had been hopelessly naïve, and perhaps to some extent it was, but there were genuine and sound reasons for believing that at the time Syria was at a turning point for the better after the ruthless dictatorship of Bashar's father, Hafez. Certainly the UK ambassador to Syria believed rapprochement was possible. Others, equally politically savvy and world weary, shared a similar outlook, only to be disillusioned when civil war later buried any hopes they might once have entertained of a turning point in relations between the west and Syria.

David Lesch, a professor of Middle East history at Trinity University in San Antonio, was one of those who had had high hopes of the new regime, having published his first book on the subject the year before the group's visit: *The New Lion of Damascus: Bashar al-Assad and Modern Syria*.[69] In a follow-up volume seven years later, Lesch sought to analyse the reasons for such a bloody and disastrous reversal with, *Syria: The Fall of the House of Assad*, concluding that Bashar just wasn't up to the task, and had succumbed to the hubris of self-delusion that he was to be his country's saviour. Hard to assess too are the malign influences of his brother, Maher, head of elite military forces, and of his powerful sister, Bushra.

In Maaloula, however, and in Christian enclaves dotted all over Syria, as they struggled to interpret Thomas' bleak 'Let us go and die with him', that was still how they saw it and prayed for it: someone who could keep the peace between Sunni and Shia Muslims, between Muslim and Christian. Everybody was 'in an unsafe situation in Syria,' Greek Melkite Patriarch, Gregory III Laham, concluded. 'It is not the fear of Islam,' he told the world, 'it's the fear of extremists. The fear is not from my neighbour the Muslim, it is from foreigners who change relations between Christians and Muslims.'[70]

It was because the British scholar, Karen Armstrong, recognised 'that people want to be religious,' but was equally aware of religion's susceptibility to be subverted by forces whose primary interest is to control and dominate, that she launched her Charter for Compassion in 2009.[71] At its heart, the Charter, which has been endorsed by the Dalai Lama among other notable figures, includes this call: 'to restore compassion to the centre of morality and religion; to return to the ancient principle that any interpretation of scripture that breeds violence, hatred or disdain is illegitimate; to ensure that youth are given accurate and respectful information about other traditions, religions and cultures; to encourage a positive appreciation of cultural and religious diversity; to cultivate an informed empathy with the suffering of all human beings – even those regarded as enemies.'

> Jesus said, 'I've mixed with all sorts of people and always let them see my human side. But their minds were too full of their own concerns to have any interest in what I had to say. My heart went out to them because they just couldn't understand. They lacked any special advantages when they came into the world and seemed determined to end their days with none. It's as if they'd been drugged. One day they'll come to their senses. Then they'll see things differently.' (GofTh 28)

At the time of writing I do not know how the civil war in Syria will end, whether, if he survives, Bashar al-Assad will be arraigned before the International Criminal Court in the Hague or have come to some accommodation with the western powers afraid of a blowback in their own backyards from jihadist extremists, and willing to tolerate his regime as the lesser of two evils. Whatever the outcome, the loss of life, the massive dislocation of those who have sought sanctuary in neighbouring states, the destruction of the fabric and much of the country's historic past, the unleashing of inter-religious mistrust, is a dreadful legacy, leading to the fear that St Takla's healing waters may by now have dried up completely.

These are lands that have known war and the rumour of war since Biblical times. Sennacherib of Syria, then Nebuchadnezzar of Babylon, both had chipped away ruthlessly, eventually wiping out Israel and colonising Judah. After them had come the Persians, and then the Greeks, the Seleucids and the Romans. This was Thomas' history, this was his people's story, this their song, and always, even in the worst of times, the belief that one day Messiah would come to free them once and for all.

And for Thomas, and the other disciples, that belief was vested in the charismatic rabbi from Nazareth, hoping they might at last be on the verge of inflicting a final defeat on the Gentile invader, only now it would herald the beginning of the end. 'And the might of the Gentile, unsmote by the sword,/Hath melted like snow in the glance of the Lord.'[72]

'Let us go and die with him' has been the cry of the Jews from time immemorial, and always the hope that this time it might be different, that this time Messiah might come, until the twentieth century, when the shame of the Shoah surpassed the worst that Thomas could have feared.

'The time to learn how to live'

'Christian theology does not know whereof it speaks,' warned the Catholic theologian, J B Metz, 'unless it recognises that it speaks after Auschwitz.' For generations the churches had peddled the false doctrine that Judaism was a failed religion, or, at best, one that prepared for and was completed in Christianity. The recovery and recognition of the Jewishness of Jesus in our time has, therefore, never been more urgent. It is why the Gospel of Thomas matters. It changes the perspective.

The Italian Jew and Holocaust survivor, Primo Levi, described how '… on the following day, the Jews would be leaving. All the Jews, without exception. Even the children, even the old, even the ill. Our destination? Nobody knew.'[73]

Now we do know. And the knowing is both painful and cathartic. The Christian record is as shocking as it is shaming. In 1215 Pope Innocent III's Lateran Council issued a directive that all Jews should be made to wear a distinctive 'badge of shame' – the forerunner of the Nazi yellow star. And in 1543 Martin Luther disseminated an outrageous tract against Jews, urging: 'Their synagogues should be burned, and whatever does not burn should be covered over with dirt so that no trace is left,' thus bequeathing Hitler a ready-made 'Mein Kampf'.

Christ has been re-crucified by his Christian followers again and again. Therefore, to say there is no Passion narrative in the

Gospel of Thomas is like saying there is no Passion narrative in the history of the Jews. It's written on their hearts and in their lives. Their history is imbued with the reality of suffering from the prophet Isaiah's 'Suffering Servant' to the twentieth-century's Shoah.

If, above all others, there is one challenge for our time in Thomas' cry and from his Gospel, it is that an open and honest reappraisal of our relationships as Christians and Jews is no longer an option.

Jesus said, 'Now is the time to learn how to live. Keep in touch with the one who lives forever. Don't wait until you die to experience life. It will be too late then to develop the art of living or to recognize God as the source of life.' (GofTh 59)

Inter-faith dialogue is never going to be easy. But to back away from it because it seems fraught with too many difficulties is to fail 'to develop the art of living,' to fail 'to recognize God as the source of life.'

The secret of all successful inter-religious dialogue is to find not only the points of overlap, but the areas of divergence too, and to realise that the strength of faiths shared is not a diminution of separate integrities but their affirmation in the cause of strengthening a shared approach to a world created and sustained by the one God. Nor at a time of a worrying increase in anti-Semitism, can we ignore the necessity to discuss the situation in the Holy Land with as much mutual respect and honesty as will be necessary. Without mutual inter-religious goodwill, the common good will be impossible to achieve or maintain. An organisation like the Council of Christians and Jews, Britain's oldest national Jewish/Christian interfaith movement with numerous local branches under the joint presidency of the Chief Rabbi and the Archbishop of Canterbury, is, therefore, a particularly useful vehicle, for addressing anti-

Semitism and promoting dialogue.

In short, we have to get away from the religious mindset that feels our revelation is so precious that other revelations are either inferior or invalid. Of course, the faith we follow by upbringing, conviction or conversion will be the one we cherish most, because it has been our spiritual window. It will be the one that has shaped our cultural and personal background, and to which we are most likely to turn for reassurance or comfort in times of crisis, or in the closing phase of our lives. But we will be missing out on a richer spirituality if we do not at least acknowledge that other ways of seeing God can also be revealing.

For all the world's great faiths, inter-religious dialogue has been a long, slow journey, but particularly so between Christians and Jews, and it is still far from over. It has been just too easy for tribes and cultures, families and nations to use their religions to emphasise their differences in the interests of dominance or conquest. Religion, because it touches on our emotional self-identity is too easily recruited as an ally to shore up our own insecurities. And until we can sit with the other, walk alongside the other, live with the other in a harmony of enjoyment and mutual uplift, having our own approach and insights expanded by the other's approach and insights, our own spirituality will be less rounded, less satisfying.

In one of her most telling challenges, British theologian and a President of the World Council of Churches, Dame Mary Tanner asserted that Christians must get away from the tendency to say to each other, 'I have no need of you'. By extension, the phrase is equally applicable in the wider context of inter-faith ecumenism. Such a phrase goes beyond recognition or acceptance, important as both of these are, to an expression that we, singly and corpo-rately, are incomplete without the other. Not in the sense of being drawn into our circle to be clones of us, but in the sense of sharing a different lens to add to the lens or lenses we already have to bring a greater clarity, to add a depth to the picture we have of God: 'the source of life'.

A recognition of the Jewishness of Jesus, of Christian shame over its subsequent relationships with its Jewish sisters and brothers, and of the issues to be addressed, important as they are, are, however, no longer enough on their own. They need widening now to include discussion and exploration with the followers of that other great monotheistic faith, Islam; a religion that draws on both Tanakh and New Testament.

Nor can discussion among the three Abrahamic faiths any longer be conducted on a one-to-one basis. There are hurts and wounds that will never be healed unless all three faiths acknowledge how inextricably inter-connected they are. The truth of the Biblical proverb that, 'If anyone is alone, an assailant may overpower him, but two can resist; and a cord of three strands is not quickly snapped', has never been more relevant.[74]

To widen the debate in this way requires us also to acknowledge that the followers of Islam are now in danger, certainly in the West, of becoming as much figures of hate as the Jews have been, and for Muslims to acknowledge that Christians are being similarly victimised in some Islamic countries.

There is 'a part of Islam in every Arab Christian,' the prize winning journalist, Anthony Shadid reminds us. 'Whatever their beliefs, they acknowledged sharing a culture that bridged faiths, joined by a common notion of custom and tradition and all that it entailed – honour, hospitality, shame, pride, dignity, and a respect for God's power. For many Muslims and Christians there was even a common origin, a fabled beginning in faraway Yemen.'[75]

When Shadid returned to trace his roots in the Lebanon, 'the call to prayer began from the Sunni mosque, faint in the predominantly Christian town but still resonant. Its lonesome, plaintive summons reached a crescendo, stopped, then began again with a declaration of the omnipotence of God.'

Changes in the demography of our Western society now

provide us with rich opportunities to realise how different cultures co-mingled can create stronger communities and a safer world. And cultures are nurtured around faiths, and faiths create cultures. When we feel confident enough to explore the resonances shared by Jews, Christians and Muslims, we may be ready to engage with the spiritual insights of Hinduism, Sikhism and the philosophies of Confucius and of the Buddha within which, and through which God has also been perceived and celebrated. How far indeed can we talk of God, as we know God, also being identified with God as others know God?

Jesus said, 'Some people have many gods. Their gods mark the presence of the true God. Where two people meet together, I'm there with them.' (GofTh 30)

– or translated literally, that, 'In the place where there are three gods, they are divine' or, 'Where there are three divinities, God is present.'

The Jewishness of Jesus can sometimes startle us into a reassessment of what faith is. It can stretch the parameters of our little boundaries. It can come at us in a way we least expect, forcing us to rethink our settled positions in a way that can shock and perhaps even disturb us deeply. There is a terrifying incertainty in a lot of what Jesus had to say, and because we have become so used to the story in the four great gospels of our New Testaments, we have become inured to their impact: an impact of sufficient force when first delivered that it led to his execution. The Gospel of Thomas shakes us out of our residual spiritual complacency to re-imagine God's New World as something much more radical than we'd allowed for, but extraordinarily magnificent in its conception.

'The results have been disappointing'
'Let us also go and die with him' still haunts and challenges our

world. But there are other ways of reading Thomas' enigmatic words.

Delve deeper and they suggest a loss of faith. Over familiar as we are with the outcome of the story of Jesus and its subsequent world-wide impact, we tend to underplay what it must have meant for Thomas and the other disciples to entertain the thought that the Jesus enterprise might end in failure; that the early expectations of that remarkable mission were unlikely to be fulfilled – at least not in the way initially expected. If we are to understand what followed, it matters that we do not try to efface this loss of hope and what it must have meant for the disciples to face the unpalatable truth that the Day of the Lord was not after all about to break into their world; that Jesus might not be God's anointed to bring it about, the long-awaited Messiah; that Thomas might be going nowhere, and that Thomas knew it!

Without an awareness of what that must have meant for them, we will not be able to appreciate the slow sapping of confidence that is the background to Thomas' story in the Fourth Gospel. The flowering of a faith of infinite complexity is only captured in the Gospel of Thomas because it has had to confront the loss of hope encapsulated in that first plaintive cry to 'go and die with him'. Both hope and the loss of hope are recognised in the Sayings. Both are natural responses to the vagaries of life. It is how one confronts the loss of hope that decides whether the outcome will be a surrender to a doomsday scenario, or to a re-appropriation of hope, albeit as something substantial rather than merely as an unwillingness to face reality. We are in a similar place. For us the loss of hope has come about as we have lost confidence that our western way of life is sustainable.

In his refreshingly unambiguous solo encyclical on the *Joy of the Gospel* (Evangelii Gaudium),[76] Pope Francis alluded to the materialism of past decades that might have wrought economic miracles, but had left in its wake a spiritual void. The Pope called it 'devastation and anguish born of a complacent and covetous heart.' Here was South American Liberation Theology applied on a world scale, and however difficult it might be to translate that into an economic system that is just and fair and serves the common good, his argument is that the Gospel requires that the case be put.

'The majority of our contemporaries are barely living from day to day, with dire consequences,' the encyclical thundered; 'a number of diseases are spreading. The hearts of many people are gripped by fear and desperation, even in the so-called rich countries. The joy of living frequently fades, lack of respect for others and violence are on the rise, and inequality is increasingly evident.' Here is a sermon that bleeds for the excluded and the marginalised 'without work, without possibilities, without any means of escape.'

These are not the benevolent musings of a naïve holy man confronted by the reality of a world in pain. These are the results of a righteous indignation born of a deep grasp of the radical theology of Jesus, which the Gospel of Thomas uncompromisingly re-presents. These are the cries of a soul that has lived and worked and made mistakes in the favela of South America, and the shanty towns of Buenos Aries.

Jesus said, ... 'The world is such a wonderful place – so much of value amongst so much poverty!' (GofTh 29b)

We are living through a time of 'epochal change,' wrote the Pope, set in motion by the enormous advances we have made in various fields of knowledge, science and technology. But he resists the easy capitalist fallback position that these things will eventually right themselves, the poor in time benefitting from the bounty of the powerful, crumbs falling from the rich man's table. 'This opinion, which has never been confirmed by the facts,' Francis warned, 'expresses a crude and naïve trust in the goodness of those wielding economic power in the sacralised workings of the prevailing economic system.' In the Pope's words, competition and a mentality based on the survival of the fittest has created a world in which, 'human beings are themselves considered consumer goods to be used and then discarded.'

Jesus said, … 'God has given humanity great resources and ability, but the results have been disappointing. We're only worth a short life.' (GofTh 85)

'Black Friday' is another disturbing indicator of the negative side of capitalism. Said to be one of the United States' most successful Christmas exports, it's the day on which consumers are tempted into shopping early with flash sales and discounts. It was estimated that half a billion pounds sterling had been spent in Britain on the first all-out UK Black Friday blitz, a figure that I found obscene, compared with the abject poverty and desperation of the displaced and the homeless across the world, let alone those in our own country, worried sick as they try to meet rising energy and food bills, and where the job market has dried up and a minimum wage is no longer a living wage.

Ours is a culture that doesn't know where it is going. The certainties we'd previously depended on to deliver a sustainable way of life, with values and institutions that could be relied on and imported across the globe, are rapidly diminishing. Hope is in rather short supply.

Jesus said, 'Our universe may suddenly come to an end and you may see it happening, but those who have God's life within them won't die.' (GofTh 111)

'A form of religion'

Underlying the sapping of hope in the institutions that we have previously relied on to deliver a sustainable future, there is also the loss of hope in any meta-narrative to frame our ambitions and to rein in our excesses. And that is the greater loss. Religion, certainly in the west, is no longer seen as shaping our lives and enlarging our 'souls'. A 2013 Survey of British Attitudes, for example, revealed that nearly half the population of Great Britain no longer identified with any religion. And it is unlikely to be any different in the USA fifty years hence, or sooner.

In past times there were always those that did not buy the religious package and, depending on the degree of sophistication that was then in play, were mostly tolerated if not accepted: the Thomas Hardys and the Matthew Arnolds, the David Humes and A J Ayers. Fine minds, and often fine spirits, who stood out from the mass as exceptions. This is no longer the case. Now, certainly in the context of western Christianity, it is the believers who are taxed with having to make the running, and the mass is becoming increasingly reluctant to conform to the patterns, and wary of the religious practices that sustained previous generations.

Equally, there seems to be a recognition that something important is being lost, with attempts to salvage the form, if not the substance, of all that religion once represented. So the popular philosopher, Alain de Botton promotes a Religion for Atheists,[77] and a couple of well-meaning entertainers launch a Sunday Assembly for people from London to Los Angeles, from Bristol to Brisbane, who want the community without the godliness.[78] These are diverting, if interesting, minority reactions to a culture that is losing its hold on faith, certainly in any institutional form, but that still yearns for companionship.

More, though, are probably in the category represented by Fran, who, while possessing an innate spirituality, is still reluctant to be too closely identified with any church. Ambivalent about organised religion in general, Fran speaks of strong feelings of not wanting to be labelled, while acknowledging 'how uncertain that sounds'. She says she prefers to remain anonymous, even admitting to feeling a bit of a fraud when attending church from time to time, and occasionally taking communion, but equally reluctant to jump into the 'I don't believe anything' camp. Open to the good in all faiths, Fran is acutely aware of the damage religions have done, and still do, opting instead to be identified with no religion in particular. 'I don't know about life after death,' she admits; 'I'm not sure what I mean by God, but the faith I was brought up in taps into something. A memory? It can still be a comfort. But more? I don't know.'

Fran's touching honesty chimes in with the analysis of the Australian academic, David Tacey. 'We are caught in a difficult moment in history,' says Tacey, 'stuck between a secular system we have outgrown and a religious system we cannot fully embrace.'[79] It is a perceptive analysis of a critical moment in the evolution of our relationship with all that we mean by God. And Fran's response to it is neither as negative as she makes out, nor as 'hope-less' as others might assume. Faith is too subtle to be packaged into simplistic definitions and precise formularies. The importance of Thomas, therefore, not least as he emerges from his collection of the Sayings of Jesus as well as in the scattered references to him in the Fourth Gospel, is that he epitomises how incertainty is the process whereby faith is explored and refined. Incertainty is not the sign of opprobrium with which conventional orthodoxy might wish to brand it, but a mark of exquisite spiritual sensitivity that resists facile attempts to confine and conform, in favour of being fully aware of the present moment whilst also remaining open to the challenge Jesus once put to the disciples:

'When you learn something which sheds new light on things, you can either act on it or ignore it. Which will you do?' (GofTh 11c)

A fascinating outcome of a survey conducted by the polling

consultancy ComRes, on behalf of the think tank Theos,[80] on the occasion of the 150th anniversary of the publication of Darwin's *Origin of Species*, found that half the British population were unconvinced by Darwinism! As someone who takes the scientific evidence for evolution for granted I found that quite starling. Proportions on this scale indicated a response much wider than could be accounted for from a creationist rump.

An interpretation that I find rather persuasive is that the reaction had less to do with what evolution implied about God as what it was thought to imply about what it means to be human. Reasonable, rational people, who take the sciences in their stride in every other aspect of their lives, baulk at the implication that we are no more than accidents of chance mutations.

That may, of course, be explained as an unwillingness to accept the judgement of Genesis that: 'Dust you are, to dust you will return.'[81] Or it may be because of an inherent conviction of a metaphysics beyond the physics – that there is an ultraviolet beyond the visible violet of the rainbow's observable spectrum, an infrared beyond the red.

Ours may be an in-between time, when it is hard to discern the way ahead, and when the best response of many is to echo the disciple's words to 'go and die with him', but it is where we are, and to deny it or condemn it is neither honest nor helpful. We are already into a new phase of human experience in which a new language is called for if we are to give fresh expression to perceptions of all we mean by God. And it must be done in a way that does not call for a suspension of our critical faculties, but that complements and enlarges them. In that respect it picks up the challenge of another of the Sayings, when:

Jesus said, 'A form of religion has grown up which has nothing to do with the Loving God. Such a pathetic faith will have to be pulled up by the roots and allowed to die.' (GofTh 40)

These are hard words for those who are afraid or reluctant to face up to the incertainties of their own beliefs, but they serve as a chilling challenge to those, perhaps subconsciously, who have been held back by a 'form of religion' which denies its essence.

Certainly, Thomas', 'Let us also go and die with him,' implies a recognition of something major changing in his and all their lives. Two millennia on, different challenges and changing circumstances require an acknowledgement that some of our inherited forms of religion may also have to be pulled up by the roots if they distort the image of God as love.

'What will happen to us in the end?'

Thomas' reaction, however, has to be read in the light of what followed when Jesus eventually got to Bethany. By then Lazarus had already been dead for days. To drive home Lazarus' actual deadness, the Fourth Gospel emphasises that Martha expected her brother's body was already in the early stages of putrefaction, ruling out any possibility of resuscitation. Nevertheless, outside the cave that was his tomb, Jesus called out his name – and Lazarus emerged from the gloom: dead man walking! It's one of those iconic images of Christian devotion that artists from Giotto to van Gogh have tried to capture, each time revealing more of themselves than of the subject. For Giotto,[82] grief and gratitude, amazement and disbelief, co-mingle to create a tableau of captivating reverence, with Mary of Bethany, conveying with her eyes, an ambiguity and multiplicity of emotions, and Jesus, authoritative and serious.

For van Gogh,[83] the image explodes with emotion. Mary is central, almost overwhelming the scene, her arms outstretched to embrace her resurrected brother, her face a tortured mixture of anxiety and barely repressed joy, while Martha is in profile, reaching forward, her hands together as though in prayer. Jesus is nowhere to be seen. Instead we are drawn to a blazing, swirling, yellow-gold sun that is such a feature of van Gogh's art:

the source of light, both natural and spiritual.

In both Giotto's and van Gogh's paintings, Lazarus is a wan figure expressing the bewilderment of someone barely awake after a long, deep sleep.

The friends of Jesus said to him, 'what will happen to us in the end?'
Jesus said, 'Why do you want to know about the end when you've
only just started? Every end depends on where you begin. If you're
lucky enough to get the beginning right, you'll discover that life is
all beginnings with no final end.' (GofTh 18)

The difficulty with reading any of the canonical Gospels is that they belong to a particular genre of writing. They may be life stories, but they are not biographies. They may deal with real incidents from the life of Jesus, but are retold to carry larger truths. Certainly there is an actual story to be told, there's dialogue to be shared, and scenes to be painted. If that is true of the Gospels in general, it is especially true of the Fourth Gospel, where Thomas is quite integral to illustrating the development of the faith experience. To read the story of the death and resurrection of Lazarus in any other way is to get lost in a forest of improbabilities. It's a story of delay and disbelief, of mixed messages and disappointed hopes, acted out against a tapestry of mourning and deeper meanings, with dialogue of extraordinary subtlety and insight. At least that's how the incident is recorded. And it's easy to dismiss it, and the spirituality that gave it credence, as unworthy of serious consideration in a rational age. But all is not as it seems, and Thomas' part in it and his reaction to it is both obvious and obtuse!

We have no way of knowing the actual sequence of events surrounding Lazarus' illness and his subsequent restoration to the family that thought they'd lost him. Our interest in such matters would be beyond the comprehension of those first-century Gospel writers. What mattered to them was the bigger meaning, of which these incidents, real as they were in their essence, were merely pointers.

This is about death and resurrection on a grand scale. This is about the nature of being. What are we here for? Where are we going? This incident in the little village of Bethany a stone's throw from Jerusalem on some unspecified day in the dim and distant past is offered to us as a way of seeing life as it might be, as it should be, here and now, on earth as in heaven, for all. It's what the Fourth Gospel does. It's the last clue to be singled out, to add to the other six.[84] It's the very opposite of 'back to the future' – it's the future projected into the present. In his hymn for a service of reconciliation in the rebuilt Coventry Cathedral – of reconciliation between former enemies in war-torn Europe – Fred Kaan sang of the need to 'remember forward to a world restored'. Thomas was not yet ready to do that. When he was, it would all fall into place.

In Yann Martel's clever, preposterously believable novel about the nature of reality, *Life of Pi*,[85] Piscine Molitor Patel (to give Pi his full name) reflects early on in the narrative that, 'We are born like Catholics, aren't we – in limbo, without religion, until some figure introduces us to God? After that meeting the matter ends for most of us. If there is a change, it is usually for the lesser than the greater; many people seem to lose God along life's way.'

And at the climax of the story, where the bureaucrats are pressing an older, wiser Pi to verify his improbable account of surviving a Pacific Ocean shipwreck in a lifeboat with only a hyena, a zebra, an orang-utan and a Royal Bengal tiger for company, Pi responds with this magnificent riposte: " I know what you want. You want a story that won't surprise you. That will confirm what you already know. That won't make you see higher or further or differently. You want a flat story. An immobile story. You want dry, yeastless factuality." Pi was having none of it, because, "The world isn't just the way it is. It is how we understand it, no? And in understanding something, we bring something to it, no?"

Outside Lazarus' tomb, Jesus wept. They were tears of distress and they were tears of indignation, shed for Mary and Martha, for Thomas and the rest, then and since, who would have to find out in their own experience that there could be no resurrection in the present or beyond, unless first there had been a dying.

As so often, T S Eliot captures the ambiguity of believing in these taut lines from *Journey of the Magi*: 'I have seen birth and death,/But had thought they were different; this Birth was/Hard and bitter agony for us, like Death, our death.'

Outside the tomb of Lazarus we can only imagine which death most occupied Thomas' thoughts. Later, he would remember the rabbi's Saying:

> *'But I do have something good to give you. It has not been seen, heard, or touched; indeed it is beyond human imagination.'* (GofTh 17)

– how far beyond, Thomas had yet to find out.

5 How did Thomas come alive?

Twin said, 'My God, it's the Leader!'[86]

IT HAPPENED FOR Thomas after he'd made a proper ending. An ending to his life as it had been; to all the hearing and the watching, to the beginning of listening and seeing. A putting away of an unreal world, of unbelievable truths, so that credible ones could be re-examined and rediscovered. A letting go of the certainties he craved so that actual incertainties could start to surface and he could repossess the reality of God, rather than the fantasy of an idolatry that passed for religion.

Psychologists tell us endings are especially important if we're to be free to move on. Endings that 'can range from an informal, pragmatic goodbye round the kitchen table, to running alongside the moving train, hands outstretched, to keep contact until the last moment'.[87] And the extent to which we're able to get on with the rest of our lives, after an ending, depends on how well we've handled that ending. And Thomas wasn't making too good a fist of it, at first, at least.

There was too much resentment, too many questions hanging in midsentence, too many inexplicables. 'For every change,' we're told, 'however much wanted there has to be an acknowledgement of some loss and an accompanying mourning.' God knows, Thomas wanted change. But not this one. Not death. And never, ever crucifixion.

What Thomas wanted, what they all prayed for, was for the coming of Messiah to bring in the promised Bright New World, to bring down the Herods and the Caesars from their thrones, and to raise up the lowly, to fill the hungry with good things and to send the rich away empty.[88] But it hadn't happened. And Thomas plumbed the depths of the full range of emotions that loss brings: 'shock, denial, disbelief; alarm, panic, anxiety; anger, protest; sadness, grief, depression.' Thomas had done the lot before he was finished.

Endings are affected by what's gone on before, and Thomas had a whole lot of unfinished business to sort through before he was ready to make a proper ending. He still had to understand that incertainties were not his curse, but his blessing; that it involved acknowledging the weaknesses, as well as the strengths of the relationship he was leaving; that Jesus could be impossible as well as irresistible, that he could be cutting, as well as tender, that God was Holy as well as forgiving. Thomas knew if he was to move on, that he'd have to see Jesus as he really was, not as he'd wanted him to be; that 'twinning' would be the clue to unlocking the secret of the mystery of God: God who was beyond all knowing and yet also known and knowable. Unless he could do that, Thomas knew he'd never be free to find himself, to become the disciple he knew he had it in him to be, and why Jesus had picked him in the first place.

For many still, their brush with religion has been so pathetically superficial that they've got stuck in the childish phase of make-believe. They are unable to handle the grown-up cut-and-thrust of the real thing, and have walked away in disgust, or sometimes with regret; unable to accept that only love can absorb the judgement of human folly and wickedness, or to believe in God alongside the possibility of our universe existing before any big bang. Whose concept of The Significant Other is so woefully defective, that when life falls apart they're left with nothing to build on.

Jesus said, 'You'll be forgiven for being an atheist, and you'll be forgiven for failing to recognise my relationship with God, but if you despise the good things that come from God you'll become so twisted that no one will be able to put you right, in this world or in any other.' (GofTh 44)

In the hours and the days following the crucifixion of Jesus, it was only because Thomas had been able to make a proper ending that it had eventually happened for him, as it had for the other disciples. He'd discovered that 'the end of all our exploring/Will be to arrive where we started/And know the place for the first time'.[89] And in Saying 113, Thomas had the perfect ending:

> *Jesus' friends asked him, 'When will God's New World come?' Jesus said, 'It won't come if you spend all your time looking for it! No one can say, 'I've got it!' or 'Look, there it is.' The New World of the Loving God is spread all over the world today, but people can't see it.'*

It summed up Thomas' carefully selected and arranged collection of his Lord's most insightful and challenging sayings comprehensively and effectively. There's certainly a sense of completion to Saying 113, an intentional deflection from unrealistic expectations and end times; a pointing to the present as the sphere of God's activity, of God's New World, not as some unattainable ideal or only for a future life, but all around us – now, to be embraced, engaged with, immersed in.

Saying 113, however, is not the one with which Thomas finished dictating his collection of some of the most intriguing and challenging Sayings passed on to him by his close friend, Jesus, because he knew he had one more Saying to record.[90] It was a Saying he could easily, and seemingly more naturally, have placed earlier at any number of appropriate points in his collection. But he hadn't, and for a reason. A clue, perhaps, that points to the way Thomas had changed from the disciple who'd once thought no further than urging his friends to 'Come, let us go and die with him', to the disciple who not only put this distinctive collection of Sayings together, but who also went on to plant the story of Jesus on the great sub-continent of India, where it holds its own to this day.

'The sum total of everything'

The links between India and Palestine can be traced as far back as king Solomon's reign. A millennium later, when Octavius Augustus ruled the western world, the caravans of the great merchant houses of the east would have been a common sight passing through Palestine on their way to Rome, laden with expensive textiles, ebony and elephant tusks, frankincense and myrrh. Shipped by Egyptian Jews from the Malabar coast to the Red Sea these oriental traders may well be the source of the account in Matthew's Gospel of astrologers from the east passing through Bethlehem when Jesus was born.[91] There was certainly a thriving trade route between the Euphrates valley and the Malabar Coast of south-west India by this time, with a well-established Jewish community in the port city of Kochi in Kerala on India's western seaboard. The route was, therefore, well established for the Christian story to find its way to India fairly early on, with the honour of bringing it there first, in the year 52 CE, being attributed to Thomas: the Apostle of the Enquiring Mind.

Today the Mar Thoma Syrian Church of Malabar has followers around the globe. And in its ancient birthplace, Indian mystics now draw on Hindu iconography to interpret Christianity, and to allow the ancient insights of the Upanishads to resonate with the vibrations of incarnation and resurrection: 'I know that Great Person of the brightness of the sun beyond darkness. Only by knowing him one goes beyond death. There is no other way to go'.[92] And Indian Christians paint pictures of 'God in human form appearing,' rising triumphantly from a lotus blossom towards a radiant light, the demon of darkness trampled underfoot:[93] Asian illustrations of words that Thomas once heard from the Semitic lips of Jesus:

I'm the light shining everywhere. I'm the sum total of everything.
(GofTh 77)

Saying 113 would have been a good place to end – with the New World of the Loving God spread all over the world. But Thomas had one more Saying up his sleeve.

'Everything is coming home to me'

Something had happened to Thomas. And it was not, as is often interpreted and implied, that his incertainties had become certainties; rather, it is that he'd realised that faith, belief, trust, which ever word you use, is of its nature something that cannot be pinned down with arithmetic exactness. It is essentially – of its very essence – to do with a different perception and awareness of oneself: the moment God breaks through. Incertainties are not aberrations to be dismissed or deficiencies in oneself to be overcome, but are themselves the signs of authenticity. It is coming to terms with that, that is transformative. It's only then that other things fall into place, like the calling forth of Lazarus from his burial cave, and the apparent 'I am' put-down to Thomas' inner scream, and the boastings of the resurrection sightings of the friends.

The Fourth Gospel frames the event in a dramatic tableau. Thomas, who'd kept missing out on whatever it was the others claimed to have experienced[94] – the woman outside the garden tomb, the couple out for a walk on a Sunday afternoon, and his mates in that upper room, now 'sees' for himself: sees, perceives, 'gets it'.

Recognise what's staring you in the face and everything else will make sense. (GofTh 5)

The Italian artist, Caravaggio reimagined the moment in oil on canvas, reinforcing the intensity of the revelation. Caravaggio, himself not yet 30, violent and brilliant, irrepressible and impossible, using his genius to give something ultimately indefinable, intuitive, ineffable, shape and form in light and shade. His painting, 'The Incredulity of Saint Thomas' now hangs in the Sanssouci museum, in Potsdam, Germany. Caravaggio's Thomas is very different from that of his later contemporary, the Spanish painter, Velasquez. Velasquez sees Thomas in profile, deep in thought, wrapped like a medieval monk in a rough habit; pensive, contemplating life's contradictions, in one hand he holds the pilgrim's staff, in the other a book. Caravaggio's portrait is almost shocking by comparison. This Thomas is more baffled than inquisitive, more dazed than defiant, a reluctant participant in a scenario he never intended, the resurrected Christ taking firm hold of his right arm to guide his finger deep inside the gaping fleshy hole in the Saviour's side. Velasquez's is probably nearer the reality, but it is Caravaggio's that is unforgettable, capturing, as it does, the incomparable climax of the Fourth Gospel's thesis, of a 'Word' that brought the whole created order into existence, through a 'Word' wrapped in a very human life, to a confession by a disciple who'd been consistently portrayed as finding faith difficult, finally confronted by the 'Word' unwrapped, free of all human constraints, but still identifiable, sentient, responding in that indelible, dramatic outburst: 'My God!'

Even so, these two gospels, the Fourth Gospel and the Gospel of Thomas, that otherwise seem to share so much in terms of capturing the original voice of Jesus, to be kindred spirits, appear at this most critical moment to part company. So some scholars have argued for reading the Fourth Gospel as a corrective to an already circulating Gospel of Thomas, to show Thomas finally 'giving up his search for experiential truth – his "unbelief" – to confess what [the Gospel of] John sees as the truth.'[95]

If, however, both gospels emerged from the same stables, then neither is an attempt to correct the other, but each offers a different angle, not on Thomas, but on Jesus himself. These two gospels may be less at odds in this final scene than passionate preachers, earnest evangelists or assiduous scholars have been wont to imply. Because the Fourth Gospel is itself a supremely intuitive text that inspires belief of the heart, whereas the Gospel of Thomas is impregnated with the Sayings of Jesus that get to the heart of that faith. We need both.

Resurrection is one of the most difficult concepts a post-modern age can be expected to entertain. Like the psychiatrist, Bion, it leads many 'to tolerate the pain and confusion of not-knowing, rather than imposing ready-made or omnipotent certainties upon an ambiguous situation or emotional challenge'.[96] Not knowing, being incertain can, however, as many following Thomas have discovered, produce the opposite effect. It can make them come alive again!

In earlier times, when our forebears lived lives more in touch with the seasons – the unpredictability of nature, of a sense of another world somehow in parallel with this one to be experienced in the so called 'thin places' – resurrection was something that was taken as given.

But then we came of age, and we lost our intuitive side in favour of a down to earth practicality. We subdued the earth, we reached for the stars. We split the atom. We released energy previously undreamed of. We cornered killer diseases. We prolonged lifespans, and in the process discarded notions of resurrection as part of our primitive, if endearing, past. So now we do not know what to do with resurrection. It's way, way outside our experience. It's not natural. 'A shock of love, it still revolts/each Easter from our shrinking crypt,' in the startling language of the young poet, Dai George.[97]

In the Port Talbot Passion, referred to in the opening chapter, Owen Sheers deals with the resurrection in terms of the annual renewal of nature after the dark cold of winter. Mary the mother of Jesus, wanting to take one last look at her dead son, finds 'he's no longer there … And in his place were flowers. It was as if someone had planted a spring meadow inside him and now, with death, it had taken bloom.' Whether for dramatic effect, or because nothing less would keep faith with the original, the three-day Passion play, nevertheless, ends with his followers looking up at an empty cross, and suddenly 'there he was … Bold as brass. He looked over us all staring up at him, and then he spoke to us. "It has begun!" he said. And he was gone.'[98]

We may identify with Jesus as somehow the human face of God. We may feel empowered by the quiet spirituality we find in a multi-layered Christian faith. We may feel fired by the righteous anger of the long ago rabbi from Nazareth to do our bit towards alleviating human misery, righting wrongs, campaigning for justice, challenging prejudice, bigotry and inequality – but resurrection eludes our rational minds.

The temptation to park it, deflect it, skirt round it is strong. But it defeats our best efforts to avoid it as it whispers in the breeze, or surfaces in the darkness of the dying, or winks in the rising sun, and we find we cannot completely forget it if we want to savour the wholeness of the Christian encounter. But how to understand it, live with it, live by it, and not be in denial of our functioning intellects? Faced with resurrection, how might Thomas, the talisman of our incertainties, offer us anything more than confirmation of those incertainties?

After my father died, my mother and I pondered the wording for his headstone. In the end we opted for words from the Fourth Gospel: 'though he die, yet shall he live.'[99] It expressed a hope based on a promise: 'he who believes in me' – from the sublime, if enigmatic, discourse between Jesus and Martha outside the tomb of her brother, Lazarus. There was a suitable element of incertainty about it that left the door open, since that 'though' is quite important – it all depends, is the subtext, on what 'believe' might mean, and what the Fourth Gospel intended, in representing Jesus, who was about to call Lazarus back to the land of the living, telling Martha: 'I am the resurrection and the life'.

At the graveside the minister or the priest will often recite the time honoured refrain: 'In sure and certain hope of the resurrection to eternal life'. But one hopes for something one cannot be certain of. One can certainly hope for something, but 'in sure and certain hope'? It is faith that gives hope its substance,[100] not the other way round!

For the first followers of the Christian way, and ever since in the mainstream of Christian belief and practice, the resurrection was never just about the return of the Nazarene rabbi seemingly alive and well. It was never the case of showing how that particular and exceptional person once, long ago, had cheated death. In the eternal engagement between good and evil, light and darkness, it was always to be interpreted as a clue, a confirmation that this dying, far from being pointless, was 'break point' – that all important moment in a tennis match when to win 'break point' changes the odds against the server.

> Jesus said, 'I'm the light, shining everywhere. I'm the sum total of everything. Everything started with me and everything is coming home to me.' (GofTh 77)

And in the Fourth Gospel we find a parallel affirmation, and made there in the context of the blind man who'd had his sight restored, which was also one of the seven clues: 'While I'm here, I supply enough light for everybody to see.'[101] And now Thomas was seeing, and 'seeing through', both in the sense of 'seeing through' to the end, the bitter end, of the journey he'd started out on when he'd urged his companions, 'Let's go', and in the sense of 'seeing through' the superficial and the temporal to the substance of what it had been about all along, and why that mattered.

In parish churches and cathedrals, week in week out compliant congregations will recite those words in the creed: 'We look for the resurrection of the dead, and the life of the world to come.' But few, I suspect, in repeating those phrases will expect decomposed or incinerated corpses to be reconstituted in physical form. Bodies are finite. Bodies have limited lifespans.

'Unless I see,' had been Thomas' perfectly reasonable objection to the boast of the other disciples. And not just see, but finger the actual wounds, the evidence of the torture and the killing. 'I won't believe that until I see the holes made by the nails in his wrists and put my finger into them. And I'll have to examine his side too!' [102]

Why be so specific? Surely not to avoid some kind of trick? Given our opportunities to view the dead we have loved and lost, we will want to see them having regained some semblance of serenity, however tortuous their end, and to believe that they are in some sense now 'at peace'. In the version of the service for the burial of the dead I invariably use, I pray that we may release our loved ones in the assurance that they are somehow now, 'safe, happy, and complete'.[103] But not Thomas. He wants to finger the holes, the tears in the flesh, the awful reality of a shameful, excruciatingly cruel and long drawn out killing. He wants to plumb the reality of that ending. Why? Because Thomas knows he can never become alive in himself unless his belief is of the heart not just of the mind – unless he can actually 'feel' it in the depth of his being.

It was the twentieth-century Anglo-Welsh writer, Glyn Jones who drew a distinction between disbelief of the heart and disbelief of the mind. 'The disbelief of the mind is awful – what you feel in youth,' he said once, 'but the disbelief of the heart in middle age, which desperately wants to believe, is ten times worse.'[104]

Disbelief of the heart is that yearning for the consolation of faith one might have had once, or wished one had. It is an awareness of an unfathomable absence that will not go away. It is a restlessness for the assurance of a recognition one needs but cannot name.

Ours is also a culture in middle age: post-modern, finding it easier to look back than forwards. It has faced the intellectual challenges of the Christian narrative, and decided either to jettison theism or to find alternative answers mature enough to sustain, rather than to undermine, faith. But now it is beset by a disbelief of the heart, and it does not know where to turn. This disbelief of the heart is ten times worse.

After the others have had their experiences of their trans-figured, transformed, lost Lord – in gardens, upper rooms, lakesides, country inns – we're told Thomas has his own unique revelation: 'My God!' – it was either the ultimate blasphemy, or it was true, the moment of Thomas' self-revelation, when Thomas not only 'gets it', but is got by it!

Thomas wants to finger the holes, to examine the side where the sword went in, but the record is significantly ambiguous when it comes to what Thomas actually did. He's invited to handle the form, but, crucially and contrary to Caravaggio's image, the account is muted on whether he actually did. It was enough that the experience, whatever it was, had got him beyond the physically tangible to the spiritually revealing, to take off clothes that were in the way in order to leave them:

'in an untidy heap on the floor', so he could *'relate to God's True Likeness without embarrassment.'* (GofTh 37b)

'Inside you and all around you'

What are these clothes that we assume and don to face the world, to disguise and conceal the imperfections of height and shape, to fend off the ravages of time, if not the barriers we erect as a buffer against too much reality? 'Go, go, go, said the bird,' in the first of T S Eliot's Four Quartets: 'human kind/cannot bear very much reality.'[105]

The analogy is different in the Fourth Gospel, there the scene is of locked doors for fear of the police, but the meaning is the same. Fears of incertainty. Of not wanting to face the obvious. Of wanting to know for sure, without realising that the knowing only comes with the letting go; the surety is always in retrospect, of the life lived, still being worked out and worked through.

Some locked doors can, of course, be useful, like those of the sanctuary, the safe place, where we can gather our breath, take the measure of our experiences, hold up the mirror without turning away in disgust or despair, secure from the pursuing demons from within and without. Inner rooms where, whether in company or alone, we can confidently explore who we are and what we're for, free from the fear of other people's or our own assumed expectations. Places where we can risk shaking down the questions that may have been floating in our heads as in a dream beyond recall, but with the lingering memory of something being amiss.

Thomas had his moment of self-awareness in such a place. An environment where the incertainties provided an opening into the mystery of God, where he was overwhelmed by the simplicity of revelation and the release of letting go: not of the questions, but of the fear of the questions, where this mature man, whether in his thirties or his fifties, finally came of age.

There are other locked doors more to do with denial than with sanctuary. More to do with clothes for power-dressing than for comfort or acceptability. More to do with the fear that unless certain received patterns are adhered to, conformed to rigidly, not only one's own existence, but the existence of all around us will collapse, and chaos ensue. It is the fear that drives the fundamentalist who needs the inviolability of a book to be sure. It panders to a very primitive fear of disorder, that when the unpredictable occurs, we must search for reasons other than the obvious, making connections that are unjustified, sometimes with appalling consequences.

So Salman Rushdie has a fatwa issued against him for writing *The Satanic Verses*, and an American pastor in Florida[106] burns copies of the Holy Qur'an, because bigots cannot handle their own sectarian incertainties, and in trying to escape from their own fears wreak havoc on those around them.

I once had an entire edition of a church magazine I was editing in my student days, bought up and pulped because an article equating the Catholic Mass with the Protestant Eucharist offended two of its readers. God save us from the insufferably self-righteous who set themselves up as God-given gatekeepers, because they cannot countenance ideas that challenge their own. What kind of God is it who has to be protected from being misinterpreted? What kind of God is it that can be brought down by a misplaced word? That is the kind of God mocked two and a half thousand years ago in the Jewish writings of the great prophets: 'One and all they are stupid and foolish, learning their nonsense from a piece of wood.'[107]

Whatever happened to Thomas in that upper room long ago, it had something specifically to do with leaving his uncomfortable ideological clothing, *'in an untidy heap on the floor'*, so that he could *'relate to God's True Likeness without embarrassment'*.

If locked doors offer sanctuary for some, and a way of hiding from reality for others, for more it may be the place they neither acknowledge nor deny. The place where the doors may not be locked but where there are unspoken expectations from within that hold them back from embracing the freedoms beyond.

Few have written with greater insight into this claustrophobic world than Marilynne Robinson, where the doors are not locked but the incertainties within and without exert a debilitating paralysis of the will. In her novel *Home*[108], she explores this territory through various relationships within and between two mid-west American clergy families, the Presbyterian Boughtons and the Congregationalist Ameses. 'Home. What kinder place could there be on earth,' muses Glory, the unmarried daughter who'd had a career and a feckless lover, but had come back and now kept house for her elderly father, 'and why did it seem to them all like exile?' It was particularly true for Jack, the prodigal son, who'd come home, but could not feel at home, and was always unlikely to stay.

This upper room of the heart, where the doors are neither locked nor open, is a place where more are held in thrall than probably realise or admit it. It's the unnatural place between action and inaction, like the boatman's anxiety in Goethe's poem, *Quiet Sea*[109]: 'Deep quiet rules the waters;/motionless, the sea reposes,/and the boatman looks about with alarm/at the smooth surfaces about him./No wind comes from any direction!/A deathly, terrible quiet!/In the vast expanse/not one wave stirs.'

Like Goethe's boatman, they are unsettled and alarmed more by the listlessness all round them, than if they'd had to battle against a gale, or keep an even keel in choppy waters: these others, trapped by their invisible ties, waiting in expectation for God to break in and to bring them their own resurrection. But they do not know how to appropriate the moment when Christ comes with the invitation and says, 'Come on, Thomas, have a good look at my hands and my side. It's okay if you want to touch!' Or, in the words Thomas remembered and wrote down in his Gospel:

> Jesus said, 'If the leaders of your community tell you God's New World is in the sky, you'll know they've got it wrong. That's where the birds will discover the New World! To say the New World is in the sky is as silly as saying it's under the sea. That's where the fish will discover it! In fact, God's New World has no precise location. It's to be found inside you and all around you.' (GofTh 3)

Resurrection appearances of various kinds and to an ever widening circle of the followers of Jesus persisted for weeks, only to come to an end with the phenomenon known as Pentecost: that infusion of spiritual exuberance that transformed their remarkable rabbi's grammar into gospel, his suffering into a sign of salvation.

'See you next'

The fishermen disciples had gone back to their old trade, with Thomas making up an extra pair of hands when work was slack. On one of those trips, we're told, they caught one hundred and fifty-three fish. The figure is precise. A night at sea without catching a thing, and then out of the blue, last thing, just before landing, a chance remark from a passer-by on the beach to try a bit further out from the rocks. A passer-by who seemed eerily familiar. A passer-by who was still there when they landed, and had a fire going so they could enjoy a hungry breakfast. It brought back memories for Thomas of that other time when the disciples had gone off in a boat on their own and been caught in a storm. This time there was no storm, but no fish either. And then this catch. And after that they were on their own again. The passer-by had passed on. But they knew. They had one hundred and fifty-three fish to show for it![110]

> The friends of Jesus said to him, 'We never know when we're going to see you next!' (GofTh 37a)

Numbers matter in the Fourth Gospel's unfolding story. The meaning is often in the numbers. Six water jars, twelve disciples. Five loaves, twelve baskets of leftovers. A sick man by a pool for thirty-eight years. To our minds this obsession with numbers is bizarre. The only way to understand it is to accept that it belongs to a style of Jewish writing current at the time the different Gospel texts were being assembled, when numbers were intended to convey the message that there was meaning in the madness.

And it was a mad time in the history of the Jews. There were constant uprisings, and within forty years of the crucifixion of Jesus on just such a charge of inciting insurrection, the whole weight of Roman power would come crashing down, bringing to an end all thoughts of national autonomy for the foreseeable future. At such a time numbers could exert a powerful hold on people's imaginations, because numbers spelled order, design, purpose. It answered the psalmist's cry, 'When will you act, Lord?',[111] with a message that might be cryptic and was never meant to be taken precisely, but 'gave the people confidence that this was indeed a significant time in history, and that history did have a meaning and a purpose with God in control of it.'[112]

For the disciples, working through the meaning of the rabbi they'd hoped had been Messiah, in the light of his crucifixion, the numbers were nothing short of apocalyptic – a revelation of resurrection. Twelve baskets of leftovers from five loaves. Twelve plus five equalled seventeen, and one hundred and fifty-three is the sum total of all the numbers up to seventeen! Before we mock this obsession with numbers, let's not forget how, for all our sophistication, we too will often renumber our houses and the floors of skyscrapers between twelve and fourteen to avoid using 'thirteen' in a pointless attempt to ward off some primitive fear of bad luck!

Numbers have exerted a strange fascination on the human imagination from the beginning of numeracy, and in the culture in which the New Testament was being assembled numbers were being increasingly used to convey esoteric messages, particularly of hope and fulfilment, as here in the Fourth Gospel. These numbers carried their own meaning, which would have been obvious to the first readers of these texts, and it was of completion, of all things ultimately coming together, of the triumph of good, of the vindication of righteousness. They conveyed a cosmic impact.

The Gospel of Thomas achieves the same result, but in a more startling way, by preserving the riddles in the teaching of Jesus. These so-called 'hidden sayings' shock us into re-engaging with a Jesus we thought we'd got signed, sealed and delivered. They force open the closed shell of our minds to rethink the crucial importance of incertainties in fathoming the divine, and living in the light of such mystery.

'Where there are no distinctions of any kind'

In an upper room long ago, according to the Fourth Gospel, Thomas had – was given – his 'My God!' moment. In his own Gospel, however, Thomas is not prepared to leave it there. There's an afterbirth to be expelled, an umbilical cord to be cut. And that's the Saying of Jesus he decides to place last. A Saying that implies an expectation that post-resurrection life does not carry on as before, but sees things differently, requires new learning. The baby must breathe on her or his own; must learn to feed so growth may follow. There is work to be done, there's a life to be lived, here and now. A life with radical consequences. God's New World is not the old one refurbished, it's a new creation: 'it *has no precise location. It's to be found inside you and all around you.'* So Thomas places this Saying last, and it is like a beginning:

> *Simon, otherwise known as Peter, said to the others, 'Mary of Magdala should leave us. "Life to the full" is not for women! Jesus said, I intend to train women like her to do all the things that men can do and to give them the same freedoms you have. Every woman who insists on equality with men is fit to be a citizen in God's New World.'* (GofTh 114)

As with most ancient manuscripts there is always speculation over whether the received text is a complete version of the original. The most discussed Gospel text to have a disputed ending is that of Mark. Had that evangelist really intended to complete his narrative on such a cliffhanger: the mystery of the resurrection left open-ended. The first witnesses, not any of the men who'd accompanied Jesus throughout his ministry, but three women, who 'said nothing about it to anyone, because they were in a state of shock ...'[113]

It's easy to see why some are tempted to rule out Saying 114 as an add-on from another source at a later date. But isn't it there, the last word in the collection, for the very reason that it was the one saying Thomas felt captured best the radical tenor of the message of Jesus? Not just that the rabbi's message was only about gender equality, though it was that, but that in its entirety it was about a wholly new way of being: God's New World.

Nor is the gender saying such a bolt from the blue. It had already been flagged up at the half-way point in the collection:

> ... Jesus said, 'I come from a place where there are no distinctions of any kind. My parent [God] taught me how to mix with everybody.' Salome said, 'You can count me as one of your friends! Jesus said, 'You and I can be friends because, like me, you have no prejudices. Prejudices make a person blind. To see clearly you must be ready to embrace all types.' (GofTh 61)

From the beginning, the radical edge of the teaching and ministry of Jesus has had to contend with the human bias towards not wanting to rock the cultural boat too much, at least not in the immediate aftermath of the crucifixion and the resurrection experience. And this final flourish in Thomas' collection is intended to be a marker on behalf of those in the early church, the one we find in formation in the Acts of the Apostles, who honoured and followed an apostleship that looked to women as much as to men for leadership and direction.

> One day Jesus saw some mothers feeding their babies at the breast. Jesus said to his friends, 'Little babies are the perfect example for those who want to be citizens of God's New World.' The friends said, 'Surely we don't have to become babies in order to qualify for the New World?'
> Jesus replied, 'When two people become one, like a mother feeding her child; when there is no difference between the way you behave

and what's going on in your mind, or between your head and your heart; when you treat males and females equally, without any distinction whatsoever; when you respond naturally to another's body language; when you accept people as they are – then you'll be ready for God's New World.' (GofTh 22)

The later history of the church failed to honour this insight allowing a patriarchal and a Greco-Roman cultural inheritance of male dominance to circumvent the radical nature of the teaching of Jesus whom they otherwise recognised and worshipped as 'God with us': Immanuel. So gender equality in the church became a no-go area, except in terms of an idealised image of womanhood: of women in supportive, deferential roles, secondary rather than primary, always handmaids never Apostles (though Mary of Bethany was one, and there were probably more)!

Every now and then an alternative voice, a rarefied spirit, might, nevertheless, cross the church's path to question the status quo, but it was not until recently that the issue became centre stage, and still divides the followers of Jesus.

One such remarkable voice within the western church who transcended the banality and pettiness of the argument because of her immersion in God, was the fourteenth-century mystic, the Mother Julian, who thought and wrote of God in uninhibited, inclusive language: 'And so I saw that God rejoices that he is our father, and God rejoices that he is our mother.' And even more radically: 'Thus Jesus Christ who does good for evil is our true mother; we have our being from him where the ground of motherhood begins, with all the sweet protection of love which follows eternally.'[114]

In his 1995 Annual Julian Lecture, the English writer and essayist, Roland Blythe, observed that, 'The Church has never been all that fond of such rare "progressives", often finding them more out on a limb and closer to God … They say: "Catch up'. …

They also say, "This is what I believe the Lord Christ is all about", judiciously adding, "by permission of Mother Church, of course"'![115] But the reality too often is that Mother Church has been none too happy to give permission. And Mother Julian's *Revelations* – believed to be the earliest surviving book written in the English language by a woman – remained largely unknown for the next six hundred years. Perhaps her sheer hiddenness as an anchorite allowed her the protection of assumed theological harmlessness!

The Gospel of Thomas matters, because it reminds us of a forgotten Jesus, the radical, progressive rabbi who tipped up the counters of the Temple's Bureau de Change, applauded Samaritans (though they were deemed mixed-race), treated women as equals, was as at home dining with unsavoury types as he was with the better off, who was without prejudice of any kind, and warned his followers that:

Prejudices make a person blind. To see clearly you must embrace all types. (GofTh 61)

The Gospel of Thomas emerges from the soil of Upper Egypt as an indictment of how easily and quickly an inclusive, world-challenging gospel can withdraw into a spurious spirituality where individual experience supplants the prophetic spirituality that Jesus lived and died for.

I have written elsewhere[116] about our resistance to facing uncomfortable truths, of our reluctance to open doors that take us out into the world as it really is, and why our spirituality depends on a refusal to fall for the illusion captured in the Seekers' sixties song: to 'build a world of our own/that no one else can share./All our sorrows we'll leave behind us there./And I know you will find/there'll be peace of mind/when we live in a world of our own.'

Reflecting on these changing times in a subsequent book, I

argue for a greater willingness to re-engage with those whose spirituality might be unfamiliar, but who nevertheless show the marks of today's 'new spiritual awakening' and are influenced 'by latent Christian belief'.

In this last title, in what has turned out to be a trilogy on contemporary spirituality, I have sought to draw these different strands together around that most misunderstood disciple, Thomas, and to dip into his remarkable Gospel to underline the critical importance of incertainty as a prerequisite for any intelligent faith that takes life, as it must be lived now, seriously. I have wanted to test the thesis that the insights of the Judaeo-Christian tradition (on which Islam also draws), with parallels in other world faiths, far from being out-dated and irrelevant in a post-modern, scientific culture, not only have some relevance in this changing theological and cultural milieu, but actually matter.

I have wanted to show that the treasure the peasant farmers turned up at a bend in the Nile more than half a century ago can provide us with a new way to appreciate the raw intensity, and the unavoidable mystery of the original message of Jesus of Nazareth; something substantial to offer us safe passage from our primitive past to a future in which a radical spirituality holds the balance between kindness and brutality. Only you, the reader, can decide if I have succeeded. If I have at least shown that incertainty is something positive, then the writing and the reflecting will have achieved their aim.

The advances we have made in empirical knowledge have blunted our capacity to be taken by surprise by those experiences and insights that are outside our post-modern terms of reference. It is too easy to dismiss the mysticism of a Mother Julian as eccentric or peculiar or too rarefied to be relevant. Even she is at pains to qualify her descriptions, for all their graphic detail: '... I saw God in an instant,' before adding, 'that is my under-standing,' and crucially, expanding it with this all-encompassing insight, 'and in seeing this I saw that he is in everything.'[117] Too often we can be too literal for our own good!

In this as in so much else, Mother Julian seems to have had an inkling that if faith is to lead us closer to God, what we label as a fault is better understood as something positive and intentional. So she singles out Thomas as one of those who had to confront their own shortcomings before they were able to appreciate the limitless love of God. So she writes that, 'God showed me that sin is not shameful to man, but his glory; for in this revelation my understanding was lifted up to heaven; and there came truly to mind David, Peter and Paul, Thomas of India and the Magdalene – how they are famous in the church on earth with their sins as their glory.'[119]

Thomas may have no narrative of the resurrection in his collection, but it is implied throughout. So when this thoughtful, vulnerable, ultimately assured disciple, and, as he describes himself, one of his Lord's *'closest friends'*, set out to pass on a collection of some of the *'most intriguing and challenging sayings'* of Jesus, there was only one place Thomas could begin, and that was with the affirmation that prefaced and inspired the whole of his Gospel, that:

Jesus is alive![119]

Appendix

The Gospel of Thomas

John Henson's translation of The Gospel of Thomas in *Good as New: a Radical Retelling of the Scriptures* (O-books 2006)

Thought-Provoking Sayings of Jesus (As recalled by Twin)
(Sayings referred to in the text are indicated by the reference number in brackets)

(1) Jesus is alive! Here is a collection of some of his most intriguing and challenging sayings, as passed on by one of his closest friends, whose real name was Jude, but better known by his nickname, Twin. Anyone who unravels these sayings and takes their truth as guide, will not experience death.

(2) Jesus said, "Make your life a quest and don't give up till you find what you're looking for. What you find may upset your prejudices, but you'll discover much to wonder at and get to grips with what the world is all about."

(3) Jesus said, "If the leaders of your community tell you God's New World is in the sky, you'll know they've got it wrong. That's where the birds will discover the New World! To say the New World is in the sky is as silly as saying it's under the sea. That's where the fish will discover it! In fact, God's New World has no precise location. It's to be found inside you and all around you."

"Other people won't understand you until you understand yourself. When you understand yourself, you'll realize you have a family relationship to the Loving God, and recognize the life of God inside you. There's no greater poverty than not understanding who and what you are."

Jesus said, "Someone who is old will have the sense to ask someone much younger about what's going on in the world today, and that up-to-date knowledge will give them a new lease of life."

"People's ideas of who is important and who isn't must be turned right around. One day, everybody's experience will be valued and be part of a shared whole."

(5) "Recognize what's staring you in the face and everything else will make sense."

The friends of Jesus asked him many questions, such as "Do you want us to do without food from time to time?" "How do we talk with God?" "What provision should we make for those in need?" "Is there any food or drink we ought to avoid?" In answer to these questions Jesus said, "If you have a feeling deep inside you that something is wrong, don't do it. Don't let your minds play tricks on you. God sees things as they really are. One day your behaviour will be seen by all for what it is."

(7) Jesus said, "Splendid are those born with the character of a wild animal who allow themselves to be tamed by tender human qualities. Disgraceful are those born with tender human qualities who choose to develop the behaviour of a wild animal."

He went on to say, "Human beings throw their nets into the sea of life and come up with all manner of fish, mostly small and worthless. Experienced fisherfolk pick out the big tasty fish and throw the rest back. If you've got ears, use them!"

Here is a story Jesus told. "One day a farmer went out onto his land with some seeds and scattered them around. Some fell on the path and the birds pecked them up right away. Some fell among the rocks and either didn't take root, or didn't find enough soil to produce full-grown plants. Some fell among the weeds and were choked; others were eaten by pests. But some fell on good soil and produced a good crop, yielding sixty or a hundred times the seed sown."

(10) Jesus said, "I've set the world on fire. I must keep fuelling it until there's a good blaze!"

(11) He said, "Everything that now exists will change – what you can see, and what you can't see."

"Being alive or dead has nothing to do with breathing and nothing to do with corpses."

"Ideas come to life when you let them shape your personality."

"When you learn something which sheds new light on things, you can either act on it or ignore it. Which will you do?"

(12) The friends of Jesus said to him, "We know you're going to leave us. What shall we do for a leader? Jesus said, "If you have any problems, you can always go to my brother James for advice. He's honest and fair. I think the world of him!"

(13) Jesus said to his friends, "How would you describe me, as compared with other people?"

Rocky[120] said, "You're like a reporter who gets the facts right."

Matthew said, "You're a deep thinker who makes good sense."

Twin said, "Teacher, I'm lost for words!"

Jesus said, "I'm not your teacher. I'm just somebody standing by the spring of knowledge, inviting people to drink. You've been over-drinking from the spring lately and getting confused." Then Jesus took Twin to one side and had a serious chat with him. When he joined the other friends again they said, "What did he say to you?" Twin said, "If I tried to tell you, you'd kill me, and then you'd be in right trouble!"

Jesus told his friends, "If you try to score points by going without food, you'll be making a big mistake. Your talk with God will be insincere and your help to those in need will be given grudgingly."

"When you visit other countries and travel around, if people invite you into their homes, eat whatever food they put in front of you. Heal any members of the household who are unwell. What goes into your mouth doesn't make you a bad person, only what comes out of it!"

Jesus said, "You shouldn't bow or curtsey to other human beings. They were all born as babies like you were. Your true parent, the one you should honour, was not born that way."

(16) Jesus said, "Some people think I'll get the peoples of the world to live together in peace in no time at all. It's not as easy as that. What I have to say will lead to deep divisions, conflict, killings and all-out war. Families will be torn apart, and individual members made to feel lonely and isolated."

(17) "But I do have something good to give you. It has not yet been seen, heard or touched; indeed it's beyond human imagination."

(18) The friends of Jesus said to him, "What will happen to us in

the end?" Jesus said, "Why do you want to know about the end when you've only just started? Every end depends on where you begin. If you're lucky enough to get the beginning right, you'll discover that life is all beginnings with no final end."

"It's good if, before you develop your personalities and ideas, you first realize how lucky you are just to be alive!"

"If you adopt my attitude to life and take to heart what I have to say, you'll learn to use the material things around you for your benefit."

"A garden has been provided for you where the trees are always green. Learn to appreciate the lovely things around you, and then, like them, you'll last forever."

The friends of Jesus said to him, "What's God's New World like?" Jesus said, "It's like a mustard seed. It begins as something very small and ends up as a large plant, big enough for the birds to roost in."

Maggie asked Jesus, "What sort of people do you want your friends to be?" Jesus told a story. "One day some children were innocently playing in a field. The farmer came along and said, "This is my field, get out of it!" The children stripped in front of the farmer to show they had stolen nothing and said, 'You can have your field, we mean you no harm!' " [Fn.1]

"Wise homeowners who've been told there's a burglar about, make sure their property is well-protected. In the same way, you must take precautions against those who would do you harm. You need an inner strength to meet the troubles that are sure to come. It helps to have an understanding friend you can talk to."

"The moment a crop is ripe, the farmer gets on with harvesting it. If you've got ears, use them!"

(22) One day Jesus saw some mothers feeding their babies at the breast. Jesus said to his friends, "Little babies are the perfect example for those who want to be citizens of God's New World." The friends said, "Surely we don't have to become babies in order to qualify for the New World?" Jesus replied, "When two people become one, like a mother feeding her child; when there's no difference between the way you behave and what's going on in your mind, or between your head and your heart; when you treat males and females equally, without any distinctions whatsoever; when you respond naturally to another's body language; when you accept people as they are, – then you'll be ready for God's New World."

(23) Jesus said, "I select my friends very carefully. I expect them to stand shoulder to shoulder with one another."

(24) The friends said, "Tell us exactly how you are thinking and feeling. We want to model ourselves on you!" Jesus said, "Trust your senses! If you're honest at heart, your honesty will help you to understand everything in the world, in the way a strong light shows everything more clearly. If you're confused inside, then everything you see will be blurred." [Fn.2]

Jesus said, "Love other people as you love yourselves. Protect their interests as keenly as you protect your own eyes."

Jesus said, "You're very good at seeing the bit of sawdust in someone else's eye, but somehow manage to miss the plank in your own eye. Only when you've dealt with your own weaknesses will you be qualified to attend to the weaknesses of others."

"Until you free yourselves from your attachment to material things, you won't be ready for God's New World. If you don't make the Rest Day a day free from life's stress, you won't be in the right frame of mind to meet with the Loving God."

Jesus said, "I've mixed with all sorts of people and always let them see my human side. But their minds were too full of their own concerns to have any interest in what I had to say. My heart went out to them because they just couldn't understand. They lacked any special advantages when they came into the world and seemed determined to end their days with none. It's as if they'd been drugged. One day they'll come to their senses. Then they'll see things differently."

(29) Jesus said, "It's very wonderful how God's Spirit brought our bodies to life. It's even more wonderful how God's Spirit can use our bodies to express herself. The world is such a wonderful place – so much of value amongst so much poverty!"

(30) Jesus said," Some people have many gods. Their gods mark the presence of the true God."

"Where two people meet together, I'm there with them. I'm also the companion of those who are on their own."

Jesus said, "God's speakers aren't appreciated where they come from. It's difficult for a doctor to be the doctor to family or close friends."

Jesus said, "A town on the top of a steep hill can be seen from all around, and it's well-protected from attack. So any truth whispered in your ear you must use every means to make public knowledge. You don't light a lamp and put it under a basket or in a cupboard. You put a lamp on a stand so that everyone coming in and going out can benefit from its light."

Jesus said, "If someone who doesn't know the district offers to show someone else the way, they'll probably both get lost!"

Jesus said, "A robber can't take possession of the house of someone strong until he's tied the strong person up. Then he can take his pick of the house's contents."

"Don't get yourself worked up about what you're going to wear to town this morning, or to a party this evening."

(37) The friends of Jesus said to him, "We never know when we're going to see you next!"

Jesus said, "When you learn to be like little children who, without feeling the least bit shy, take off all their clothes and leave them in an untidy heap on the floor, then you'll relate to God's True Likeness without embarrassment."

(38) Jesus said, "You've enjoyed listening to the many things I've had to say to you. I've told you what no one else can tell you. Make the most of the opportunities you have to get my advice. There will be times when you won't be able to get hold of me."

Jesus said, "The members of the strict set have taken away the keys of knowledge and hidden them. They're not interested in the truth themselves and do their best to make sure no one else has access to it either. You can only outwit them by being as crafty as snakes and harmless as pigeons."

(40) Jesus said, "A form of religion has grown up which has nothing to do with the Loving God. Such a pathetic faith will have to be pulled up by the roots and allowed to die."

Jesus said, "If you offer what you have to others, you'll find you have more to offer, if you have nothing to offer, you'll end up with nothing,"

Jesus said, "Keep on the move."

(43) The friends of Jesus said to him, "We'd like to know who you really are. Where have you got your ideas from?" Jesus said, "It seems you've not yet recognized me by what I say to you. Some of you are like people who claim loyalty to God without being interested in what God says, and some of you are like those who discuss what God says without being interested in God."

(44) Jesus said, "You'll be forgiven for being an atheist, and you'll be forgiven for failing to recognize my relationship with God, but if you despise the good things that come from God's Spirit you'll become so twisted that no one will be able to put you right, in this world or in any other."

Jesus said, "You're no more likely to have a good time with prickly people than you are to find your favourite fruit in a bed of thistles. It's as if we each have a cupboard inside us. Good people bring out good things from their cupboard, but bad people have only nasty things to offer from theirs. You can spot a bad person from the way they talk about others."

Jesus said, "From the dawn of humanity until now, there has not been a better example of how we are meant to be than John the Dipper. He's someone we can all look up to. But, as I've told you before, anyone who becomes a citizen of God's New World by becoming as innocent as a child, will be of even greater value to humankind than John."

Jesus said, "You can't ride two horses at once or aim for two different targets at the same time. You must make up your mind where your loyalty lies. Anyone used to drinking vintage wine will not be enthusiastic about cheap table wine. You don't put new wine into dirty old bottles. You'd ruin the wine that way! You don't patch a new shirt with a piece of rag taken from an old shirt. It wouldn't look right!"

"If two people in a family or a community redirect the energy they've been wasting on fighting each other into working together in harmony, there's no limit to what they'll be able to achieve."

Jesus said, "Do you sometimes feel you're the only one who loves God? Cheer up; God's pleased with you! Your heart belongs in God's New World. You'll meet up with the others there."

(50) Jesus said, "If anyone asks you, 'Where do you come from? Where do you get your ideas?' you should reply, 'We come from the light which appeared at the beginning of all things. That same light has made us what we are.' If they ask you, 'Are you the light itself?' you must say, 'No, we're only children of the light, people who know the living God as our parent.' And if they ask you, 'What evidence can you give us of your family likeness to God,' say 'Like God we're always on the move and always at rest.' "

(51) The friends of Jesus asked him, "When will those who have died be at peace, and when will God's New World come?" Jesus said, "It's all happened already; you just can't see it!"

The friends said, "We've counted over two dozen of God's speakers who spoke about you in times past." Jesus said, "They are no longer relevant. I don't know why you bother with them when you have among you someone who's right up-to-date!"

The friends of Jesus asked him, "Should males have their foreskins cut to conform with our tradition?" Jesus said, "If it were so important, boys would be born without their foreskins. There's more to be gained by removing restrictions of the mind and heart."

(54) Jesus said, "The poorest people count most in God's eyes. They're already citizens of God's New World."

(56) Jesus said, "Unless you escape from the patterns of thought and conduct given to you by your parents; unless you develop your own personality, distinct from your brothers and sisters; unless you become truly adult and take full responsibility for your actions, as I've done, you won't be fit to be a member of my team."

Jesus said, "You must get to know all about the world in order to discover how empty it is. Anyone who has experienced that emptiness is ready to be a first-class citizen!"

(57) Jesus said, "Here is a picture of the Loving God's New World. A farmer sowed his seed, but during the night, someone who didn't like the farmer very much sowed weeds among the seed. The farmer didn't let his workers pull the weeds up, but said, 'If you try to pull up the weeds, you'll pull up the wheat with them. When the crop is ready to harvest, it will be easy to spot the weeds. They can be sorted out then and put on the compost heap.'"

Jesus said, "People who've had a hard life are the ones who count in God's eyes. They know what life's all about."

(59) Jesus said, "Now is the time to learn how to live. Keep in touch with the one who lives forever. Don't wait until you die to

experience life. It will be too late then to develop the art of living or to recognize God as the source of life."

(60) Jesus drew the attention of his friends to someone from another country who was on the road to Jerusalem and carrying a lamb. Jesus asked them, "Why has he got the lamb tied up?" They said. "Probably because he means to kill it and have it to eat." Jesus said, "He won't get any food from the lamb until he's killed it." "That's obvious!" they said. Jesus said, "If you have no wish to give yourselves for the life of others, like a lamb, then you'd better find yourselves a secure hideout. There's no security in making yourself comfortable with a friend on a sofa. At any moment one of you will be taken out for execution and the other spared." [Fn.3]

(61) Sally said, "Who are you, Sir? You've shared a sofa with me and eaten from my table as if you were used to moving among the ruling classes!" Jesus said, "I come from a place where there are no distinctions of any kind. My parent taught me how to mix with everybody." Sally said, "You can count me as one of your friends!" Jesus said, "You and I can be friends because, like me, you have no prejudices. Prejudices rob people of their sight. To see clearly you must be ready to embrace all types."

(62) Jesus said, "To understand the things I say, you need to use your imagination."

Jesus said, "Don't disclose secrets of a personal nature to those you can't trust."

Here are some stories Jesus told.

(63) *(i)* "There was once a man who came into a large amount of money. He decided to buy a farm. He planned to equip it with the

latest machinery, buy the best seed for planting and build some new barns to store the crops. He thought, 'It will be a good investment and I'll be able to look forward to a comfortable old age.' The very night after he'd made this decision, he died." Jesus said, "If you've got ears, use them."

(64) *(ii)* "A business woman was planning a dinner party. When she had fixed a date and made all the preparations, she sent a member of her office staff to the business premises of each of her colleagues, with a personal invitation. The first one he called on said, 'I'm having trouble at the moment getting money back from some of my debtors. I've arranged to meet them the day of the dinner party. I'm sorry, I won't be able to come.' The next one said, 'I've bought a new house and we're moving the furniture in that day. I'm sorry I won't have time for the party.' The third one to get the invitation said, 'My friend is getting married that day. I'm the best man and I've got to arrange the wedding breakfast and the dance afterwards. No chance of my getting to your dinner, I'm afraid!' The last one the messenger called on said, 'Your boss has chosen an inconvenient date. That's the day I always collect the rents from my tenants. Thanks for the invitation all the same.' When the man got back to the office, he said to his boss, 'None of them are coming. They're all too busy and send their apologies.' She said. 'Let's have some fun. Go out on the streets and invite some interesting characters to share my meal. It will be good to talk about something other than work for a change!' Jesus said, "People who devote their whole lives to possessions or making money don't appreciate the good things my parent has to offer."

(65) (iii) "A landowner let out his property to tenant farmers who agreed to supply him with a proportion of the produce as rent. When he sent his agent to collect what was due to him, they grabbed hold of him, beat him up and very nearly killed him.

When he reported to the landowner what had happened, the landowner said, 'Perhaps they didn't know who you were.' When he tried again with another agent, the same thing happened. The next time, the landowner sent his son. He said, 'Perhaps they'll show a bit of respect for my son.' But the farmers, realizing they had the heir to the estates in their hands, beat him to death." Jesus said, "If you've got ears, use them!"

Jesus said, "That stone the builders couldn't get to fit anywhere – put it where it's going to get noticed. It's the keystone. It will hold the whole building together!"

Jesus said. "Those who are highly educated but haven't learnt to understand themselves don't know very much at all."

Jesus said, "Think yourselves lucky when you're hated and persecuted. You'll find a secret place of peace where nothing can touch you. Those whose persecution comes in the form of anxiety are lucky too. They'll come close to the mind and heart of the Loving God."

Jesus said, "Well done those who go without food in order to provide food for those whose stomachs are empty!"

Jesus said, "If you use your natural gifts and talents to the full, you'll lead a worthwhile life. If you don't have that urge to make the very best of yourself, you'll shrivel up and die."

(71) Jesus said, "I'm going to bring about a revolution which no one can reverse!"

A man said to Jesus, "My brothers have stolen my share of the family property. Tell them to give it to me." Jesus said, "I'm sorry friend, I don't know anything about property rights." Then Jesus turned to his followers and said, "I'm not a lawyer, am I? I work out in the fields, bringing in the harvest. I'm looking at a bumper crop, but I need more help. Ask the owner of the estate to hire some more workers. It's a matter of urgency!" The man said, "It seems to me there are many standing round the bar waiting for a drink, but the tap's run dry!" Jesus said, "I'd put it another way. At a party there are always some who nervously huddle together near the door, but only those who take that lonely step and walk right in enjoy the fun!"

Jesus said, "The New World of the Loving God is like someone who kept a well-stocked jeweller's shop. One day she came across a very fine pearl. She had a keen eye to the value of things, so she sold up all her stock to become the owner of the pearl. You should be like her and go for the things of highest value which stand the test of time."

(77) Jesus said, "I'm the light, shining everywhere. I'm the sum total of everything. Everything started with me and everything is coming home to me. Split a piece of wood and you'll see me there; lift up a stone and you'll find me there."

Jesus said, "Why have you chosen the country for your day out? Who do you expect to see? A politician who sways with the popular mood? Someone wearing the latest court fashions? Your rulers may be well-dressed, but they're not very bright!"

A woman who was listening to all this said, "I bet your mother's proud of you. I'd be, if I were your mother!" Jesus said, "Save your kind remarks for those who do what the Loving God asks them to do! The time's coming when it will be better to be without children."

Jesus said, "When someone comes to grips with what life is all about, they will also understand the part their own bodies have to play in the scheme of things. People who are at ease with life and at ease with their bodies are very rare and should be highly valued."

Jesus said, "People get to positions of power by means of their wealth. But real power is being able to cast wealth and position aside. In God's New World, those who sit by me have places near the fire, but those who keep their distance from me are out in the cold."

(83) Jesus said, "You can see what someone looks like on the outside, but their relationship to God is hidden and mysterious. It's impossible to know what God looks like. The sight is too bright for our eyes. But God's character can shine through human beings."

"You like looking at your faces in a mirror. But when you get a picture of God's pattern and purpose for you, you see how much room there is for improvement!"

(85) God has given humanity great resources and ability, but the results have been disappointing. We're only worth a short life."

Jesus said, "Foxes have holes they can bolt to and birds can fly up to their nests, but humanity has no place of rest. It's part of being human to feel frustrated because we're limited by what our bodies can do, but some people allow their personalities to be completely taken over by their physical needs, and that's really tragic."

Jesus said, "Be grateful to those who bring the good things God has intended for you. You should do your best for them in return. Indeed, you should say, 'When are they going to come this way again so we can reward them as they deserve?'"

Jesus said, "I notice some of you religious people washing the outside of your cups. It's obvious you're only interested in outward appearances. It's time you realized that God, our maker, is concerned about what goes on inside us as much as how things look on the outside."

Jesus said, "If you let me be your friend, I'll teach you to relax. I'm a carpenter by trade. The yokes I make for oxen are smooth and light. I'm a teacher too and I don't bully my pupils. You'll be at ease with me."

(91) The people listening said, "Who are you exactly? How can we trust you when we don't know anything about you?"

Jesus said, "You're very sharp in your observation of the world of nature, but you've not observed me very closely. You're not even aware of the challenge I'm giving you this very moment. (92) If you have open and inquisitive minds, you'll get the answers you're looking for. It's true that in the past I sometimes dodged your questions. Now that I'm offering you the answers, you've lost your curiosity. (93) You're fond of saying, 'You can't preach to a dog or teach a pig its lessons.' Make sure those words don't apply to you! Those who explore discover; those who knock get invited in."

Jesus said, "If you've got money to spare, don't lend it at an interest. It's better to give your money freely to someone you don't expect to give it back."

Jesus said, "The New World of the Loving God is like someone making bread. They take a little yeast and put it in the dough and it produces many large loaves of bread. If you've got ears, use them!"

(97) "God's New World is like someone walking from the shop with a bag of flour. They haven't noticed there's a big hole in the bottom of the bag, and they leave a long trail of wasted flour behind them. Imagine how they feel when they get home."

"God's New World is like someone preparing to run the Marathon. First they put themselves to the test on practice runs. Then when the day of the big race comes, they'll be able to complete the course."

(99) The friends of Jesus said to him, "Your brothers and your mother are waiting for you outside." Jesus said, "Those here who are doing what the Loving God wants are my true family. They will be citizens of God's New World. Like me, my followers must grow up and break free from the ideas they got from their parents. They must learn to love their true mother, God's Spirit. She is the one who gave me life."

Somebody showed Jesus a large coin and said, "The Emperor's agents make us pay our taxes." Jesus said, "Give the Emperor what belongs to the Emperor, give God what belongs to God, and give me what belongs to me!"

Jesus said this about the strict set, "I wish those Holy Joes would get lost! They're like the dog in the manger. They don't eat what's there and don't let the cows eat! You're lucky if you realize the strict set are out to rob you of the good things you're enjoying. Be ready to defeat their arguments."

Once some members of the strict set said to Jesus, "We're having a day of prayer and fasting, will you join us?" Jesus said, "Why? What have I done wrong? What have your spies caught me at?

There's no need to stop eating until the party's over. That will be the time to go without food and to ask for God's help."

(105) Jesus said, "If, like me, you know your Mum and Dad, then, like me, they'll call you a bastard!"

(106) Jesus said, "You'll be truly human when you learn to live in harmony. Then you'll overcome all obstacles."

Jesus said, "God's New World is like a shepherd who owned a hundred sheep. The fattest of them wandered off, so the shepherd left the other ninety-nine and searched for the fat one until he found it. Because he'd gone to all that trouble, he said to the sheep he'd rescued, 'I love you more than all the others put together!'"

Jesus said, "Those who show me affection will share my character and I'll identify myself completely with them. They'll get to know the secrets of my heart."

Jesus said, "God's New World is like a farmer who didn't know that one of the fields belonging to the farm had treasure buried in it. When the farmer died, the property went to the next of kin. The treasure still remained undiscovered. Then the heir sold the field. The new owner ploughed the field, discovered the treasure and was able to finance the projects of others." (So those who've made good use of their time in the world to make valuable discoveries, should share them.)

(111) Jesus said, "Our universe may suddenly come to an end and you may see it happening, but those who have God's life within them won't die." (Remember Jesus said that those who've honestly come to terms with themselves are worth more than all the world!)

Jesus said, 'It's sad when people cannot relax their bodies because their minds are full of hang-ups, and it's sad when people cannot think straight because of the demands of their bodies."

(113) Jesus's friends asked him, "When will God's New World come?" Jesus said, "It won't come if you spend all your time looking for it! No one can say, 'I've got it!' or 'Look, there it is.' The New World of the Loving God is spread all over the world today, but people can't see it."

(114) Simon, otherwise known as 'Rocky', said to the others, "Maggie should leave us. 'Life to the full' is not for women!" Jesus said, "I intend to train women like Maggie to do all the things that men can do and to give them the same freedoms you have. Every woman who insists on equality with men is fit to be a citizen in God's New World."

Endnotes

1. *Good as New* overcomes some of the obscurity of 'standard' translations by adopting a 'contextual translation' method. 'The Greek can never be translated word for word,' Henson explains in his Introduction to *Good as New*. 'Neither should it be translated sentence by sentence, or even in some instances paragraph by paragraph. Sometimes the scripture writers developed what they wished to say over longer sections.'

   This is particularly true in the case of the Gospel of Thomas.

2. Mark 3:14 Revised English Bible (REB, Oxford University Press, 1989)

3. Cf Isaiah 9:11

4. Mark 6:3 & Matthew 13:55 REB, where the variant 'Judas' is used.

5. Where Thomas is said to have built a palace for King Gondophares.

6. Lynn Bauman: The Gospel of Thomas: Wisdom of the Twin (White Cloud Press, Second Edition 2012)

7. Wisdom of Solomon 7: 26 REB. The whole section from 7.22 to 8.1 is a reminder of how deeply rooted many apparently distinctive Christian interpretations are in Jewish literature and theology. What else does it mean for Paul to describe Jesus in 1 Corinthians, as 'the power of God and the wisdom of God' (1:24, REB)?

8. Quoted in the National Theatre Wales' launch programme for April 2011.

9. The script was made available to participants on a day to day basis, but has now been published as a complete volume as The Gospel of Us by Owen Sheers (Seren, 2012)

10. Wolfhart Pennenberg : Jesus, God and Man, (Philadelphia: Westminster Press, 1968)

11. Mark 15: 40 REB

12. Philippians 4: 8 REB

13. Christian Wiman: My Bright Abyss: Meditation of a Modern Believer (Farrar, Straus and Giroux, 2013)

14. John 20:25 REB

15. John 20:25 REB

16. Alan E Lewis: Between Cross and Resurrection (Eerdmans, 2000), p 45

17. Cf John 2: 1-11

18. Cf John 4: 46-54

19. Cf John 5: 1-8

20. Mark 9: 19 REB. An almost identical version can be found in Matthew and in Luke's gospels.

21. Marvin Meyer: The Gospel of Thomas: The Hidden Sayings of Jesus (Harper Collins, 1992)

22. See James M Robinson, Professor of Religion at Claremont Graduate School's description in The Discovery of the Nag Hammadi Codices, The Biblical Archeologist, vol 42, No 4, (Autumn 1979)

23. denouncing any who 'tried to counter the preaching of the truth by preaching the knowledge which is falsely so called' – from Eusebius's 4th century History, iii 32.8

24. Donna Leon: A Question of Belief (Arrow books, 2011)

25. 2 Thessalonians 5:21 Good as New version. The text was the motto of my old Oxford college.

26. Walford Davies in the notes to Penguin's selected poems (2000)

27. Reform Magazine, October 2013

28. Beowulf in Seamus Heaney's translation (Norton, 2000)

29. Baptists and the Communion of Saints: A Theology of Covenanted Disciples (Baylor University Press, 2014), chapter 4.

30. Genesis 1: 31 REB

31. Michael Nazir Ali, Triple Jeopardy for the West (Bloomsbury,

2012)

32. Rowan Williams, Faith in the Public Square (Bloomsbury, 2012)

33. Brian Moore, The Colour of Blood (Jonathan Cape, 1987)

34. Exodus 19: 6 REB

35. Cf John 9: 1-7

36. Cf John 6: 5-14

37. Cf John 6:16-24

38. John 14: 5

39. Luke 22:16

40. John 14: 2-5, Good as New translation

41. A collaborative project between Cardiff Reform Synagogue and Butetown History & Arts Centre (2012)

42. From Chana Bloch and Stephen Mitchell's translation of The Selected Poetry of Yehuda Amichai, New York (Harper & Row, 1986)

43. John 13:36 REB

44. John 11: 16 in the Good as New version

45. The Bell Jar (Heinemann, 1963) end of chapter 9.

46. Edvard Munch's iconic painting

47. The Bell Jar, beginning of chapter 20

48. McCarthy, Cormac, The Road (Knopf, 2006)

49. Saunders Lewis is generally regarded as the greatest figure in the Welsh literature of the twentieth century: the T S Eliot of Welsh letters. In its final form, his play, 'Blodeuwedd' was published in 1948 (by Gwasg Gee).

50. Sioned Davies: The Mabinogion, Oxford, 2007

51. speaking in 1993 on the findings of the Pontifical Council of Science.

52. Alister E McGrath's definition of spirituality in Christian Theology: an Introduction (Wiley-Blackwell, 5th edition, 2011)

53. Mark Ravenhill's translation, theatre programme note

54. Richard Dowden on Eliza Griswold (FT 19&20/02/11)

55. Spirituality or Religion? Do we have to choose? (O-books, 2009) chapter 8

56. Alister E McGrath: ibid (beginning of chapter 11)

57. The Qur'an, Surah 50: 16 in M A S Abdel Haleem's translation (Oxford World Classics, 2004)

58. Rumi, Masnavi i Man'avi, the spiritual couplets of Maula

59. As the Canadian theologian, Stuart Brown, describes it.

60. Arabia Through the Looking Glass (Fontana, 1980)

61. The Ramayana: book 2

62. Arcadia Books, Ltd, 2000

63. from an address to a joint session of the United Reformed Church Mission Council and the Methodist Council, October 2012. See also Cornick's 'Letting God be God' (Orbis 2008): 'The sheer otherness of God means that no space is sacred, for God is the elusive absence in the midst of all that is sacred.' (p104)

64. Psalm 8: 5 REB

65. Quoted in Eusebius

66. John 8:12 REB

67. John 12: 36 REB

68. John 11: 16

69. David Lesch: The New Lion of Damascus: Bashar al-Assad and Modern Syria (Yale, 2013)

70. The Tablet, 21 Sept 2013

71. For which Karen Armstrong won the prestigious TED prize. TED describes itself as 'a clearinghouse of free knowledge from the world's most inspired thinkers.'

72. Lord Byron: The Destruction of Sennacherib

73. Primo Levi, Survival in Auschwitz, English translation, (Barnes & Noble, 1947)

74. Ecclesiastes 4: 12 REB

75. Shadid, Anthony: House of Stone (Houghton Mifflin, 2012)

76. The complete document can be read via: www.the tablet.co.uk

77. 2012 (Hamish Hamilton, 2011)
78. Sunday Assembly, founded by Sanderson Jones and Pippa Evans, the i newspaper: November 2013
79. The Spirituality Revolution: the Emergence of Contemporary Spirituality, Melbourne and Sydney: (HarperCollins, 2003)
80. See theosthinktank.co.uk for 2009
81. Genesis 3: 19 REB
82. In the Scrvegni Chapel in Padua
83. In the Van Gogh Museum, Amsterdam, Netherlands
84. Ref: the incidents as re-imagined in chapter 2: What did Thomas doubt?
85. Yan Martel: Life of Pi (Canongate, 2002) chapter 16
86. John 20:28 Good as New version
87. Chris Butler and Victoria Joyce: Counselling Couples in Relationship (John Wiley & Sons, 1998)
88. cf The Magnificat, Luke 1:52 and 53
89. T S Eliot: from the last of Four Quartets, Little Gidding (Faber & Faber, 1944)
90. It is thought Thomas dictated his collection to a market place scribe in modern day Urfa, south-east Turkey, the Athens of the East in first century CE
91. Matthew 2:1 and following
92. Brhadaranyaka Upanishad — I.iii.28
93. See the work of the artist theologian Solomon Rah
94. John 20: 11 and following & Luke 24:13 and following
95. Pagels, Elaine. Beyond Belief: The Secret Gospel of Thomas (New York, Vintage, 2004)
96. Bion, ibid.
97. From his poem 'Towards the Palatability of Contemporary Faith in 'The Claims Office' (Seren, 2013).
98. Sheers: The Gospel of Us, ibid.
99. John 11:25 RSV
100. Hebrews 11:1 REB

101. John 9: 5 Good as New

102. John 20: 25 Good as New

103. Contemporary Prayers for Public Worship, Coates, Gregory, Micklem, Wren, et al. (SCM 1967)

104. Glyn Jones: The Dragon Has Two Tongues (University of Wales Press, 1968)

105. T S Eliot: Four Quartets, ibid.

106. Pastor Terry Jones in 2011 in the sanctuary of his Dove World Outreach Center in Florida, USA

107. Jeremiah 10: 8 REB

108. Home, p 294 (Macmillan, 2008)

109. Set to music by Schubert. Scott Horton's translation.

110. John 21:11REB

111. Psalm 6: 3 REB

112. John Holdsworth: The Old Testament (SCM Study Guide, 2005)

113. Mark 16: 8 Good as New translation

114. Revelations of Divine from Love, the long text, 59

115. Published by The Friends of Julian of Norwich, e-mail: TheJulianCentre@ukgateway.net

116. See 'Spirituality or Religion' & 'Seeing the Good in Unfamiliar Spiritualities', ibid.

117. From the Short Text, 8.

118. From the Short Text, 17.

119. Saying 1

120. Readers will notice that in my text I have reverted throughout to the more familiar names for ease of identity – author.

Acknowledgements

I am indebted to my old college friend, John Henson, for encouraging comments on my first draft, offering invaluable suggestions on contents and vocabulary, and especially for permission to reproduce his translation of The Gospel of Thomas. Particular thanks are also due to Dr Phil George, who found time to read the revised draft with the care of an editor, and whose incisive questions, both theological and literary, have helped to clarify and to amplify my argument. I am equally indebted to those others who read through the manuscript and offered generous and supportive endorsements and to the John Hunt publishing team for taking up the manuscript and daring to believe in it initially.

Thanks are also due to my friend Stephen Raw, textual artist and designer, for the cover design, and to Anna Williams, the librarian at St Michael's College, Llandaff, for assistance with locating sources relating to the discovery at Nag Hammadi; to Rabbi Monique Mayer for signposting sources on the observance of Passover prior to the fall of Jerusalem, to Kim Fabricius for ensuring I revisited Caravaggio and introducing me to the writing of Christopher Wiman, to my daughter, Ellen, for her interests and encouragement throughout the writing process, and to my son, Owain, for successfully retrieving an erroneously discarded chapter from my computer!

First and foremost, though, I owe more than I can say to my wife, Denise, who, unsuspecting, has influenced the core of this book much more than she realises, as well as proofreading various versions of the manuscript and reining in my tendency to write over-long sentences!

Responsibility for the interpretation and argument in the final version, though, must inevitably rest solely with me.

Sources

Every effort has been made to acknowledge sources where known. Any errors or omissions will be readily acknowledged in subsequent reprints.

Biblical references, other than those from the Good as New translation, are from the Revised English Bible (Oxford University Press and Cambridge University Press, 1989).

Abraham-Williams, Gethin: Spirituality or Religion: Do we have to choose? (O-books, 2008) & Seeing the Good in Unfamiliar Spiritualities (circle books, 2011)

Armstrong, Karen: A Short History of Myth (Canongate, 2005)

Bailey, Kenneth E: Jesus Through Middle Eastern Eyes: Cultural Studies in the Gospels (SPCK, 2008)

Bauman, Lynn: The Gospel of Thomas: Wisdom of the Twin, second edition (While Cloud Press, 2012)

Bloch, Chana & Mitchell, Stephen: The Selected Poetry of Yehuda Amichair (Harper & Row, 1986)

Botton, Alain de: Religion for Atheists (Hamish Hamilton, 2011)

Butler, Chris and Joyce, Victoria: Counselling Couples in Relationships (John Wiley & Sons, 1998)

Brown Stuart: The Nearest in Affection: Towards a Christian Understanding of Islam (WCC. 1994)

Coates, Gregory, Micklem, Wren, et al: Contemporary Prayers for Public Worship (SCM, 1967)

Cornick, David: Letting God be God: The Reformed Tradition (DLT, 2008)

Davies, Sioned: The Mabinogion (Oxford, 2007)

Eliot, T S: Four Quartets (Faber and Faber, 1944)

Eusebius: Ecclesiastical History (Digireads, 2005)

Fiddes, Paul S, Haymes, Brian & Kidd, Richard: Baptists and the Communion of Saints: A Theology of Covenanted Disciples

(Baylor University Press, 2014)

George, Dai: The Claims Office (Seren, 2013)

Heaney, Seamus: Beowulf (Norton, 2000)

Henson, J. C.: Good as New: a Radical Retelling of the Scriptures (o-books, 2004)

Holdsworth, John: The Old Testament (SCM, 2005)

Jones, Glyn: The Dragon Has Two Tongues (1968) & Selected poems 1946-1986 (University of Wales Press, 2000)

Julian of Norwich: Revelations of Divine Love (Penguin Classics, 1998)

Lesch, David: The New Lion of Damascus: Bashar al-Assad and Modern Syria (Yale, 2005) & The Fall of the House of Assad (Yale, 2013)

Leon, Donna: A Question of Belief (arrow books, 2011))

Levi, Primo: Survival in Auschwitz (Barnes & Noble, 1947)

Lewis, Alan E: Between Cross and Resurrection: a Theology of Holy Saturday (Eerdmans, 2001)

McCarthy, Cormac, The Road (Knopf, 2006)

McGrath, Alister E: Christian Theology, fifth edition (Wiley-Blackwell, 2011)

Martel: Life of Pi (Canongate, 2002)

Meyer, Marvin: The Gospel of Thomas: The Hidden Sayings of Jesus (Harper Collins 1992)

Moore, Brian: The Colour of Blood (Jonathan Cape, 1987)

Nazir Ali, Michael: Triple Jeopardy for the West (Bloomsbury, 2012)

Pagels, Elaine. Beyond Belief: The Secret Gospel of Thomas (Vintage, 2004)

Plath, Sylvia: The Bell Jar (Heinemann, 1963)

Raban, Jonathan: Arabia Through the Looking Glass (Fontana, 1980)

Robinson, J M: The Discovery of the Nag Hammadi Codices (The Biblical Archeologist, vol 42, No 4, Autumn 1979)

Robinson, Marilynne: Home (Farrar, Straus & Giroux, 2008)

Ross, Hugh McGregor: Jesus untouched by the Church (Sessions, 1998)

Russell, Gerard: Heirs to Forgotten Kingdoms: Journeys into the Disappearing Religions of the Middle East (Simon & Schuster, 2014)

Shadid, Anthony: House of Stone (Houghton Mifflin, 2012)

Sheers, Owen: The Gospel of Us (Seren, 2012)

Tacey, David: The Spirituality Revolution (Harper Collins, 2003)

Thomas, Dylan: Selected Poems (Penguin Classics, 2000)

van Unnik, W. C.: Newly Discovered Gnostic Writings: Studies in Biblical Theology No 30 (SCM, 1960)

Weinandy, Thomas G: Easter Saturday and the Suffering of God (International Journal of Systematic Theology, Vol 5, No 1, March 2003)

Williams, Rowan: Faith in the Public Square (Bloomsbury, 2012)

Wiman, Christian: My Bright Abyss: Meditation of a Modern Believer (Farrar, Straus and Giroux, 2013)

Also by Gethin Abraham-Williams

Spirituality or Religion? Do we have to choose?
(O-books)

Religion is out and spirituality is in. Certainly for Kate, a hospital consultant, religion had become something of a problem. It was buried deep in a letter between friends, as if the admitting was no light thing, but had to be hacked and mined out of the more inaccessible seams of her being. 'I cannot feel comfortable in the Church here,' she revealed. 'It is very routine and unimaginative. Also I begin to feel a bit of a heretic these days – I am a follower of Christ's teaching and philosophy; I believe in a God (a concept I do not find easy or even wish to describe in concrete terms). However, I do not even feel the need for all the complex ideas of "God made man", "redemption", etc. I am comforted to realise that some theologians agree.'

Kate had thinkers in mind like Professor Keith Ward, the popular and respected Christian academic in Oxford, honest enough to say that 'to become Christians, we seem to have to take on board a very complicated philosophy and become involved about angels on the heads of pins,' and 'it is all very confusing and not very relevant.'

Simon Barrow, Co-Director Ekklesia
reconnects rhetoric with reality

Tony Campolo, Eastern University, Pennsylvania
not only has it good things to say, but is brilliantly written

Keith Clements, former General Secretary Conference of European Churches
touches a real contemporary nerve

Davis Coffey OBE, President, Baptist World Alliance
a generous and adventurous book

Martin Conway, former President, Selly Oak Colleges, Birmingham
explores the spiritual dimension in an illuminating way

David Cornick, General Secretary, Churches Together in England
this wise, generous and humane book cannot fail to enrich and enlarge our understanding of the ways of God with human beings

Robert Ellis, Principal, Regent's Park College, Oxford
packed with insights that will encourage those tempted to give up on religion

John Henson, New Testament translator
has an important message for the 21st century

Eley McAinsh, Director, Living Spirituality Network
a challenging and provocative book

Rt Revd Cledan Mears, formerly Bishop of Bangor
compelling and refreshing

Barry Morgan, Archbishop of Wales
a book that will stretch our minds and imaginations and also move our hearts

Joan Puls OSF, former Superior General, Sisters of St Francis, USA
I recommend this thought-provoking book to anyone who is a disciple and a seeker

John Rackley, former President Baptist Union of Great Britain
written in a lyrical style that beguiles what it explores, there is a sharpness of analysis beneath the surface that is not satisfied with easy answers

Mike Starkey, Church Times
wisely retorts that 'religion' and 'spirituality' as popularly used are simplistic and unhelpful

Mark Tully, Presenter Something Understood, BBC Radio 4
featured in the To Change or Not to Change broadcast

Hilary Wakeman, Editor, Open Spirituality N/L (Ireland)
wrestles creatively with the question in its title

Seeing the Good in Unfamiliar Spiritualities
(Circle-Books)

I do not know if there is such a thing as the God-gene, or if some brains are hard-wired to respond more readily to ideas of God. I only know that if God is, then God is for all and not for the few.

I do not know why some of the most ethereal spiritual music has been produced by composers who describe themselves as unbelieving but I am grateful that their work has allowed my spirit to soar.

I do not know why some of the most spiritual and the most thoughtful people I know, find my believing strange, but I am glad of their friendship.

I do not know what it means to think of God against the immeasurable vastness of the universe, any more than I can account for the problem of evil on earth, but I think it must all be of a piece.

I do not know how some who say they believe as I believe, can behave in ways I find abhorrent, but I will walk with them as long as they will walk with me, as I will walk with God, and believe God walks with me.

I do not know how spirituality works, I only know that, for me, God helps make sense of life, and explains me to myself.

I cannot define or explain who or why God is, I cannot imagine God, but I sense I can trace the characteristics of God in the man who was baptised in the Jordan and transcended all religions.

Gregory A Barker, the University of Wales: Trinity Saint David
This important little book dares to address some of the most pressing issues of our time ... without tired dogmas but with powerful images that release one's imagination.

Simon Barrow, co-director Ekklesia
... offers a stimulating and necessarily provocative interpretation of what is happening in a mixed-belief society and how we might respond.

Myra N Blyth, Tutor, Oxford University
Inspired by the writings of the Hebrew prophet Ezekiel, this book promises to become a spiritual classic in our time and deserves to be widely read.

Lavinia Byrne, religious commentator and author
An intriguing account, rooted in the author's biblical knowledge and drawing on his rich experience as a practitioner.

Ian Fosten, Reform magazine
A timely word for Christians who are challenged by the huge variety of religious and spiritual experience in Britain today.

The Furrow, the Journal of the Contemporary Church
... the subject matter of this short book is particularly pertinent in our generation.

Lee Harmon, The Dubious Disciple Book Review
***** This book is a joy to read, and one to fill our dreams with hope.

Murdoch MacKenzie, Iona: Coracle Reviews
Celtic mysticism laced with the poetic genius of the author.

Barry Morgan, Archbishop of Wales
... a book that could help many who want an intelligent and creative faith.

Diarmuid O'Murchu, author of *Ancestral Grace*, etc
... rich in insight, wisdom and hope. A treasured resource as we journey through today's changing spiritual landscape.

+ Samuel Poyntz, Church of Ireland Gazette

... both impressed and moved by the chapter dealing with merc –
merciless and merciful.

CHRISTIAN
ALTERNATIVE

Throughout the two thousand years of Christian tradition there have been, and still are, groups and individuals that exist in the margins and upon the edge of faith. But in Christianity's contrapuntal history it has often been these outcasts and pioneers that have forged contemporary orthodoxy out of former radicalism as belief evolves to engage with and encompass the ever-changing social and scientific realities. Real faith lies not in the comfortable certainties of the Orthodox, but somewhere in a half-glimpsed hinterland on the dirt track to Emmaus, where the Death of God meets the Resurrection, where the supernatural Christ meets the historical Jesus, and where the revolution liberates both the oppressed and the oppressors.

Welcome to Christian Alternative... a space at the edge where the light shines through.